Paycheck to Paycheck to Millionaire

The Path to Wealth and Financial Freedom. Learn the Unshakeable Habits for Success and Prosperity

Napier Clark

© Copyright 2019 - All rights reserved.

The content contained within this book may not be reproduced, duplicated or transmitted without direct written permission from the author or the publisher.

Under no circumstances will any blame or legal responsibility be held against the publisher, or author, for any damages, reparation, or monetary loss due to the information contained within this book. Either directly or indirectly.

Legal Notice:
This book is copyright protected. This book is only for personal use. You cannot amend, distribute, sell, use, quote or paraphrase any part, or the content within this book, without the consent of the author or publisher.

Disclaimer Notice:

Please note the information contained within this document is for educational and entertainment purposes only. All effort has been executed to present accurate, up to date, and reliable, complete information. No warranties of any kind are declared or implied. Readers acknowledge that the author is not engaging in the rendering of legal, financial, medical or professional advice. The content within this book has been derived from various sources. Please consult a licensed professional before attempting any techniques outlined in this book.

By reading this document, the reader agrees that under no circumstances is the author responsible for any losses, direct or indirect, which are incurred as a result of the use of information contained within this document, including, but not limited to, — errors, omissions, or inaccuracies.

Contents

Introduction _____ 1

Chapter 1:
Mindset _____ 4

Chapter 2:
Stop Buying Lottery Tickets _____ 23

Chapter 3:
The Power of a Goal _____ 33

Chapter 4:
No Plan B, Only Plan A _____ 42

Chapter 5:
Life's not Fair _____ 48

Chapter 6:
You're Going to Die _____ 58

Chapter 7:
Never Be Satisfied _____ 68

Chapter 8:
Go Big or Go Home _____ 75

Chapter 9:
Positive Optimism _____ 86

Chapter 10:
Haters Criticism _____ 95

Chapter 11:
Never Tap Out _____ 102

Chapter 12:
Millionaire Success Hacks _____ 113

Chapter 13:
The Challenge_____ 127

PAYCHECK TO PAYCHECK TO MILLIONAIRE

The Path to Wealth and Financial Freedom. Learn the Unshakeable Habits for Success and Prosperity

---

NAPIER CLARK

Introduction

To be successful, you need to achieve your goals, and to achieve the goals you set you need to have a positive mindset. Unfortunately, the failure to achieve set goals leaves many of us feeling disappointed and depressed which drives us to give up on the goals entirely. Success requires definite goals and the commitment and desire to realize the goals. Success cannot be achieved overnight; it is paramount that you know that it is a time-consuming process that requires hard work and patience to be successful.

To be among the few who succeed, you should know how to achieve your goals, and you must take the pursuit of success seriously. There are those who do not set goals at all but still hope to achieve the things they want- they certainly get some of the results they want but find most of their desires elusive because they do not have a plan. They pursue their goals by groping in the dark, which is frustrating, uncertain and tiring.

Paycheck to Paycheck to Millionaire

Success begins with finding a purpose, then defining and identifying specific goals to help you attain the purpose, and then mapping out a detailed action plan to guide and help you achieve the purpose.

Do you want to be successful in life? Do you want to achieve everything that you always wanted to? If your answers are yes, this book is exactly what you need right now! As you flip through the pages, you will find detailed insight on everything that you've ever wanted to know about being successful in life.

So, if you're really looking to make it big in life and achieve things that are practically impossible for others, give this book a try! It'll give you great insights on how to achieve and sustain success.

By following the insights in this book and going after your goals daily, you will develop and master the success elements you need to achieve your goals. Achieving your goals is not easy, and you will indeed be faced with some trying moments, however, through self-belief, positivity, and by following a clear action plan, you will have the commitment, focus, resilience and will to achieve everything you set out to do. Additionally, you will learn to apply the success tenets to overcome the inertia which often stifles goals even before you begin pursuing them.

You have probably heard this before, that success is all about the mindset –the person with the right mindset will get what he or she wants while those with a fickle mental attitude will almost always fail.

Napier Clark

Our thoughts determine whether we shall succeed at something or not; you basically have the power to decide what direction and how high your achievements are going to be.

Chapter 1:
Mindset

What is success to you?

Most people have different definitions of success, but they all boil down to how happy they are, how healthy they are and how much wealth they have. One way to be successful is to have a positive mindset. This means that you must believe that you are capable of the success that you desire and that you have beliefs that can support and sustain your success. It does not really matter how hard you work to obtain wealth; if you do not have positive beliefs about money, then wealth will always seem to be moving away from you.

Many people desire wealth but have negative beliefs about money. This is partly due to their subconscious mind. In order to understand this, you need to understand that your mind isn't just one unified clamp of cells that sits atop your shoulders. It has three main parts, the conscious mind, the subconscious mind, and the superconscious mind. The superconscious mind is sometimes referred to as the universal mind. It contains the collective knowledge of humanity and is the source of imagination and inspiration.

Napier Clark

The subconscious mind can be likened to the operating system of a computer. It contains most of our programs and beliefs that direct how we behave, what we believe and is responsible for storing our habits and our memories. The conscious mind is the rational part of you that evaluates life and is always trying to solve problems. It's the part that is normally 'talking' in our heads (for example, when you are reading without vocalizing) and is always jumping from idea to idea. When you desire to change your life, it is easy to make the decision consciously, but this rarely sticks. It is only by bringing your subconscious mind on board that you can create lasting change.

The subconscious mind mostly contains ideas, memories, and beliefs that we acquire when we are children. This is because, at that stage, we had no way of knowing if what our elders told us was true or not, and we accepted their ideas without questioning. This is bad because we sometimes acquire negative beliefs from people who meant well but did not know any better. For example, if your parents believed and told you that they had always been poor and that getting money was hard, then unless you come to refute those beliefs, they will continue to be true to your life. What your subconscious believes normally becomes your reality.

The best thing about the subconscious mind is that it does not rationalize. If you come to change those beliefs in adulthood and believe for example, that you can become wealthy, the moment your subconscious accepts it, your reality will begin to alter to match your new beliefs. This, however, means that you must work hard at uprooting any negative beliefs that you may have about health, wealth and happiness and begin to actively install beliefs that are in line with the kind of life you desire. The best decision you can make for yourself is to take an active role in directing your life. This means you begin to analyze your life and the beliefs that you hold and begin disputing negative beliefs and installing new ones in line with who you want to be.

For many people, they begin to realize the negative beliefs they have when they find out what they want and begin to actively pursue it. When you discover your purpose, you begin to change how you think about your life. If you decide to pursue this purpose, normally it requires that you develop strong beliefs in yourself and begin to actively change your life so that the achievement of your dreams is possible. This change in perspective and priorities are sometimes so radical that people change who they are completely to become the kind of people who can achieve their dreams.

Anything Is Possible

It is not yet known what the full capabilities of a human being are. We use a very small percentage of our brain, and even the world's geniuses do not come close to utilizing half of their brain capacity. What this implies is that we are capable of a great deal more than we think we are. Normally the only limits we have are the ones we place on ourselves. As far as life is concerned, anything is possible.

Consider how Olympic records get broken time and time again, even though we always think we have reached the threshold of speed. Consider all the people who change their circumstances, rise above the obstacles they encounter and thrive even at times when change is considered impossible. What about all the companies that begin and succeed during economic depressions. What this implies is that you define what is impossible in your life. Whatever you decide is impossible, you will never go past it until you change what you believe.

Have A Purpose

We have talked about how having a purpose may propel you to make great changes in your life. Having a purpose is sometimes defined as having a 'why.' Your purpose is the product of your passions and your values. When you have a passion for something, it means you have a strong emotional drive towards pursuing and accomplishing that thing. Most of the time, the difference between the tasks you perform excellently at and the tasks that you are subpar at is how much passion you had towards the task. For example, a teacher who is passionate about teaching may go above what may be required of them to ensure that their students succeed while one without the passion may do the bare minimum

Your values are based on what you believe is important, particularly in terms of morals and beliefs. Examples of values include honesty, integrity, excellence, kindness, and freedom. Your values help clarify what you are willing to do and how you behave. For example, a person who values freedom may be more inclined towards self-employment opportunities while one who values honesty will be dissuaded from jobs that do not follow this value for example, stealing. You can very easily define your purpose if you take your passions and your values into account. There are many benefits of knowing your purpose and some of them are discussed below.

- Having a purpose clarifies your direction. Having a purpose may be likened to having a map of where you are going.

- Your purpose helps you maintain your focus on the goals you want to achieve.

- Having a purpose is the first step in creating a plan. Unless you know where you are going, you cannot create a plan to go there.

- Having a purpose helps in avoiding distractions. You are less likely to engage in harmful and useless behaviors when you have a purpose you are actively pursuing.

- A purpose is a remedy for confusion. Confusion stems from having a directionless life.

- A purpose is useful in living a life you enjoy. If you are following your passions, then you will enjoy the pursuit of your dreams.

- A purpose allows you to live a congruent life. A congruent life is one that is in alignment with what you value and what you believe.

- A purpose is useful in making day to day decisions as it allows you to distinguish between what is important and what isn't.

- Having a purpose helps you define your commitments and motivates you to act.

Why You Need a Life Purpose

A Purpose Is the Starting Point of The Life You Are Meant to Live

A life purpose is the first step to living the life that you are meant to live. Without a purpose, your life is basically an aimless unfocused pursuit of many unclear goals- you can live a life chasing goals which in the end turn out to be an illusion, something you do not want.

With a life purpose, you consciously pursue what you really want despite the challenges there may be, with the full knowledge and commitment to what you want to achieve in the long run. A purpose will lead to the right goals, an actionable plan and deliberate steps for a meaningful life.

A Clear Understanding of What Is Important

The point here is really about priority- a purpose helps you decipher what is important and what is not. Many times, we do not really know what is important and what is not because we do not have a clear understanding of what our purpose is. We do not know what we are really meant to do; therefore, we do not know how to prioritize our goals.

To Give Meaning to Life
Without a doubt, when you have a purpose, you have the 'why' for your life- you have the meaning of life. Purpose gives your life a clear direction and meaning which means that you will achieve more as compared to running around without a purpose. A life with meaning is a happier and healthier life with better odds of success.

Drive and Focus
A purpose is a passion. When you are on a journey to achieve a purpose, you will be filled with enthusiasm and passion for attaining it. With passion, you get an inextinguishable drive and focus on staying on course and jumping any hurdles that get in the way of achieving your life purpose. Purpose boosts performance and energy physically and mentally to pursue your goals and ultimately realize your vision.

Success
Success is about doing the right thing to achieve what you want. What better guide to success than a clear purpose! Instead of seeking success unto itself, find your purpose and use it to succeed—direct your energy to do what you like and make success a reality by doing what makes you happy. Discovering your true purpose is the easiest and surest way to success.

A purpose is a powerful part of our being, and once you identify what your purpose is, nothing can really stop you from achieving any height of success. Therefore, before you begin setting any goals, you need to find out what your purpose is in life because by pursuing what you are passionate about your chances of success are raised exponentially. If you are not happy with what you are doing or are feeling empty and aimless with your goals, it is probable that you have not pinpointed what your purpose truly is.

How to Discover Your Purpose?

Like we have discussed above, your purpose should be something that you are interested in and are enthused about. It is very difficult to commit to a purpose which you do not like. Here is a short process which you can use to find your purpose

Interrogate Your Abilities and Strengths

We innately have a deep purpose in us which we can and should discover. All you need to do it to discover what it is that you are meant to do and achieve, and you will have discovered your purpose. People have different purposes based on interests and abilities- you only must discover where your strengths are. That is why in the creation of wealth, for example, there are varied ways of how people make money- artists, lawyers, doctors, sportsmen, etc.

In other words, the result is success money wise; however, the means of getting there is really a purpose which it either a talent skill, interest, etc. Ask yourself the following questions as you explore your abilities and strengths- what you love doing and what comes to you effortlessly. Your purpose should be something that makes you happy and does not require you to struggle to do.

Identify Your Top Expressed Qualities and How You Enjoy Expressing Them

You already know that you are born with your purpose which is lying latently awaiting activation to help you realize your vision and to help you succeed. Therefore, in finding your purpose, you should identify the top qualities you possess, your strengths, and how you most enjoy using or express them. In your top qualities or strengths lies your life purpose, and in how you best express them lies the foundation on which to base your goals and vision.

Create Purpose Mantra

A purpose mantra is basically a personal statement to describe your vision to always remind you of what you are meant to achieve. Mantras are very powerful tools that will not only remind you of your target but will also ensure that you have a positive mindset to believe and commit to your goals and purpose.

Follow Your Instincts

There is no more accurate and reliable guide in whatever you do than your instinct. Your inner guide is always correct and is something that you must consult and listen to always as you identify and commit to purpose. It will navigate the path to your purpose and help you work through your goals to get you there. Your inner voice will plot a reliable map for you to follow to reach your destination successfully.

How to Have A Mindset for Success

It is now quite clear that you need to have a positive mindset in order to be successful. You may now ask what can be considered a positive mindset. Generally, we can consider two main types of mindsets. People normally have either one in different categories of their life, and it determines how successful they are.

There is a growth mindset and a fixed mindset. A growth mindset is a future-oriented mindset while a fixed mindset is past-oriented. A person with a growth mindset believes that their lives can change, that they can go after the things they desire and that they can grow, learn and adapt. On the other hand, a person with a fixed mindset does not believe that they can change, learn, grow or adapt. In order to achieve success, you must have a growth mindset.

Develop A Positive Mindset

Unwavering commitment requires a positive mindset more than anything else, yet it remains one of the most challenging habits to master. In fact, a lack of the right mindset is the number one reason why many of us will not achieve our goals. A positive mindset will help you to pursue your goals relentlessly- it gives you the ability to get back on track and to learn from failures. To be successful, you must believe that you can succeed.

How to Create A Positive Mindset?

Once we know our life's purpose, we can them begin to form and nurture a positive mindset to help us achieve the goals we set to reach our purpose. The power of positive thinking is incredible; if you hope for the best and look forward to good times, then you will have a happier, less stressful and successful life.

Positive thinking is a mental state where one expects to get favorable outcomes in whatever they do. Positive thinking therefore means that you actively train your mind to bear creative thoughts that transform energy into reality. We are what we think- by allowing negative thoughts and fears to rule your mind, you are destined to be captive to the ensuing pressures.

The first thing you must do to attain positive thoughts is to stop dwelling on your failures and put more emphasis on your successes. Highlight and concentrate on your accomplishments at work and use the things that did not turn out as expected purely as lessons for future endeavors. Failures are not supposed to weigh you down; they are supposed to make you better and stronger; they are lessons or reference points but not condemnation.

Studies and research have proved that those who practice positive thinking are more successful at goal setting. Achieving goals and realizing our life's purpose is not possible without the right mental attitude to align our abilities and focus on what we set out to do. A positive mindset will give you direction and purpose. Unfortunately, many of us have trouble tuning and focusing our minds to help us reach our purpose. A positive mindset will give you the best chance of reaching your goals.

Goal setting and success without a positive mindset and the resultant drive to achieve your goals leads to failure, and that is why many of us never achieve what we set out to do. It is because we do not know or omit to cultivate a positive mindset required to chase our goals successfully. If you do not develop a positive mindset you will struggle to overcome the challenges of pursuing your goals. A positive mindset is what will keep you going by enabling you to concentrate on the positives, however difficult things get, and will help you to pursue and visualize your goals for success.

Having a positive mindset for success begins with changing your environment to reflect your purpose and vision- it is impossible to sustain a positive mindset in a negative environment. You start by improving your immediate physical surrounding. So, how do you become a positive thinker?

The only way to be successful at positive thinking is to be able to tell what a negative thought is and to work at keeping them at bay. Examples of negativity or negative thoughts are:

- If you find yourself sieving out positive aspects of a situation and dwelling on the negative. For example, you are complimented at work for completing an assignment ahead of time then instead of enjoying the compliment; you instead embark on thinking of ways to even finish your assignments faster than you did.

- You take the blame for everything bad that happens. When a problem arises, you are quick to blame yourself even for things you ought not to beat yourself over.

- Living in fear of a catastrophe by always expecting the worst to come your way. You get soiled by a car splashing rainwater on the road, and you automatically decide that your day is doomed. You condemn yourself to have a bad day.

- You are a prisoner of perfection. Nothing is worth your while unless it is perfect and things in your world are either bad or good with nothing in between.

How to Focus Positivity in Your Mind?

Positive People

Start your shift to a positive mindset with the people around you get rid of negative who will be toxic to your plans and purpose and replace them with like-minded people who understand what you are working at and will advise, encourage and support you. Replace negative people with those who will help you with your weaknesses and complement your strengths.

Positive Surroundings

Since mindset is about thoughts, you want to be in a surrounding which will conjure positive thoughts and feelings to enable a positive mindset that will ensure that you are mentally relaxed, creative and high performing to realize your vision. Your surroundings should inspire and motivate you.

Clean up your space and get rid of clutter, light up your space with natural lighting to boost brain function, and have vision boards to remind you of your goals and what you need to do.

Positive Thoughts

Your mind is the most important tool in the journey to success and wealth creation, and if your mind is not tuned for success, you cannot achieve any of your goals. A positive mindset requires positive thoughts which will spawn positive habits which lead to actions aligned to pursuing the goals you set and creates a goal oriented subconscious to imprint your purpose and vision in your thoughts.

Distinguish the negative aspects of your thinking and areas of your job that need changing. Identify the poisonous areas and work towards changing them; begin being more hopeful and optimistic.

Evaluate your thoughts by having a periodical assessment of your mindset throughout your workday. If you discover your mind is harboring negative thoughts, redirect your thought to more positive things.

Take it easy. Do not be too uptight or sad to allow yourself moments of joy. You need to laugh even more during and about the difficult things you may be facing. Laughter reduces stress.

Be a self-motivator by always encouraging yourself. Look at the positive side of everything and always be optimistic.

Positive habits are integral to attaining goals- they keep you on track and suppress negative ways. Develop positive habits is easy and all it requires is consistency. Creating a success mindset requires you to be repetitive and consistent with positive mindset habits. Remember, your thoughts create the things you want and the person you will be.

Developing a positive mindset is critical for success because, without a success mindset, you cannot take the steps required to achieve your goals especially when things become challenging. Developing a positive mindset is not something that can be done overnight; it takes time, practice and habituation to master. Remember that you are introducing into your life something that is completely alien.

Commitment and persistence are really the fuel that will keep you pursuing your goals and are integral for success. By developing an unrelenting commitment to achieving a goal, any challenges, obstacles and even failures that you meet along the way can easily be overcome. The belief and commitment you have for your life purpose should constantly feed and ignite in you the desire to succeed.

Besides the characteristics of a growth mindset mentioned above, there are other components of a growth mindset that increase your chances of attaining success. These are:

Having A Plan
Human beings are goal oriented. We find fulfillment by overcoming challenges and adapting. Whenever we are rudderless, we have a tendency towards depression and confusion, but when we are actively planning and executing on our goals, we find joy and fulfillment. Self-actualization is the highest need in Maslow's hierarchy of needs. Self-actualization refers to the fulfillment of the potential a person has.

According to Maslow, self-actualization is a vital motivator after the motivation to fulfill one's physiological needs (food, clothing, shelter, love, and belonging). Some theories of human development also find that contentment in old age comes as a result of looking back at your life and finding that you have made significant life accomplishments.

Having Good Relationships
Human beings are social creatures. When it comes to becoming rich, there are two main ways of gaining wealth: providing a service that solves people's problems or providing art. The wealth you desire is in

the hands of other people and the methods are the main ways to obtain it. Relationships are important because we are the sum of the people we stay around. When you have a growth mindset, it is important to stay around people who have the same view of life as you so that you may grow together.

Having Perseverance

A person with a fixed mindset focuses on the failure, a person with a growth mindset focusses on the process, and the lessons learned. Life is defined by what you do just as much as it is determined by how well you persevere. The more challenges you face and overcome in the course of attaining your dreams, the more fulfilled you will be. In life, there is no such thing as smooth sailing. In fact, the most absolute thing about life is that it is always changing. You must learn to adapt to the new changes if you desire to grow.

Perseverance is witnessed before a business begins its operations and throughout the course of its operations. We should not be afraid of facing challenges or failing rather we should be afraid of remaining the same. This is because it means you are not really growing. Positive relationships are vital when it comes to perseverance. You need people who will keep cheering you on as you go through life's speed bumps. Don't forget to be your own biggest cheerleader too.

The Willingness to Learn

They say there is nothing new under the sun. If you have an idea you wish to implement in order to be successful and achieve wealth, there is probably someone out there who had a similar idea. There are two kinds of people generally, those who learn from their mistakes and those who learn from the mistakes of others.

We live in a digital era which reduces our planet to a digital village. You have two choices, you can go through the long way of learning, or you can fast track yourself and therefore fail smarter and better. Learning does not guarantee that you will not make any mistakes, it just ensures that you avoid those mistakes that you can.

How to Make Decisions to Help You Achieve Your Goals?

In order to achieve success, you need to make just one decision, to go after what it is that you desire. This is only possible if you know that which you desire (you have a purpose) and then creating an actionable plan and following it through so that you make your dreams a reality. The best way to make sure that you can achieve your goals is to write them down. If you consistently focus on your goals, you will be able to start making progress on your dreams which brings you closer to success.

If you desire to be successful in your life, you will need to have a positive mindset. Believe that what you desire is possible for you. We live in a limitless universe that rewards hard work and focused attention. All you must do is to decide once and for all. Find your purpose, make actionable plans, execute, review and repeat until you accomplish what you desire.

You have a choice when it comes to your mindsets and belief. The next time a problem arises in your time, stop and analyze your first reactions. Are they characteristic of a growth mindset or a fixed mindset? always Take responsibility for your own mindset and decide today to have a positive mindset.

Chapter 2:
Stop Buying Lottery Tickets

In the pursuit of wealth, there is a certain appeal to shortcuts. Take a lottery ticket for example, while it may cost you just a little money, you can win millions. However, it is also an easy way of losing money. When you are broke or short of funds, it is easy to fantasize that you will be a winner (and you can), but there is a reason this is a fantasy.

First, the odds are not in your favor. The odds get lower and lower depending on the number of digits you must pick and the range of these digits. Compounded by the fact that you may have to participate severally leading to spending more money you don't have to buy more lottery tickets and it really makes no sense why you would participate in the lottery.

Lottery tickets can also be any silver bullets you think could get you to those riches faster. From gambling to get rich quick schemes, there is a whole industry that preys on individuals who desire money now. They gain more from you than you do from them.

You May Ask, Then What Can I Do?

The best and safest bet you have is to be prepared to do actual work. You must pick one plan that you think will work and then you must focus on it until it succeeds or until experience proves that it won't in which case you discard it. If you desire success, stop spending your hard-earned money on fantasies and get to work.

The Foundation of Success Is Hard Work

Anyone who desires success must be ready to pay the price for it and many times the price is simply to work hard. Working hard for success may be defined as the diligence to pursue and complete tasks geared towards achieving a goal or set of goals which will enable the attainment of success. We live in an era that may not value hard work as much as it values smart work. Smart work means analyzing the tasks that you are meant to do and concentrating on the tasks that move you forward the most.

A lot of people work hard every day, but they work on the mundane, monotonous tasks rather than giving priority to the tasks that have the most impact. While you will still work hard, you will be selective about where you put your effort. All references to hard work shall, therefore, refer to diligent, focused, smart work. When working hard, there are some important things you need to do.

It is important that you dream big and you set goals. It is on these goals that you work hard. It is useless to commit to toiling every day with no end goal in mind. In fact, it is impossible to separate important work from unimportant work if you do not have criteria from which to judge your tasks. When you have goals, you must break them down into daily, and weekly action plans. This process of breaking down goals involves analyzing what tasks will get you ahead faster and assigning them to yourself daily. Work hard comes in by ensuring that you stick to this plan no matter what. It is vital that you decide, and you commit to it.

When you have a goal, it is not deciding that pushes you to work on your goal but the commitment to the result. You must commit to the plan you have and to the daily actions you have decided are important. If you have decided to start a business and you determine that it's important that you read about business management and financial management every day, it is your commitment to read every day that will improve your knowledge. After all, many people decide on goals every New Year's Day, but very few people stay committed to the decision. Commitment also increases your endurance when things go wrong because you refuse to be defeated. In the end, it's the ones who commit that succeed

If you want to be successful, you must be ready to gain experience. Some people get caught in a learning trap. They want to be perfect before they start. They spend days planning, reading and generally trying to prevent any problems they think they will encounter that they never actually go out and gain experience. While it is not bad to want to be ready, the future is uncertain, and at some point, you will have to do the actual work. Remind yourself that obstacles are inevitable, but they are not fatal. You must be ready to fail a few times in the process of becoming better. You may have as much theoretical knowledge as you desire, but it will never be worth more than experience.

You need to be willing to network. Go out and meet people who are working in the same field as you. If you are brave, you can even visit those that are against your ideas. Those in your line will share with you what they know and what they have done that has worked while those against your ideas will push you to think of ways to expand your brand so that they too may benefit. Keep in mind, however, that you can't please everyone.

In the process of networking, you will be able to make healthy relationships with different people. You can learn all you wish to learn and be an expert in your field but remember the money you want is with other people. When you are out there making meaningful connections, you increase your chances of success compared to when you stay in isolation.

Importance of Hard Work
Hard work leads to results which serve as a basis for evaluation. When you begin to work hard towards a goal, you begin to start making progress. In the process of executing your plans, you may encounter stumbling blocks, and you may fail a few times. With the right

mindset, you can transform these failures into teachable moments. Look for the lesson to be learned from the failure and then course correct so that you increase your chances of success. If you are not making progress, then you have no way of knowing what parts of your plan work and what parts don't.

Hard work creates opportunities. Deliberate, consistent action towards your goal allows you to gain experience which you can share particularly with those of like mind. In this process, you get opportunities to learn and to meet people for example partners, investors and customers. People are normally very willing to help, but they can't help you if you are seated on your couch doing nothing. You can take your idea to someone who is doing it on a larger scale, and they may be willing to help you, but only if they see that you have potential, you know what you are doing and that you are hard working. You don't need to be an expert to approach the pros, but don't expect that they will have the time to teach you everything

Working hard teaches you useful values. Hard work is a good value to learn, but you can also learn time management, consistency, persistence, excellence, etc. These values are useful in day to day life, and they affect how people view you. If you are trying to create a brand, for example, a business, these values are also reflected in your brand, and if they are good, they will attract people. Some people find that they don't have to spend a lot on marketing themselves because their good values market themselves through word of mouth. After all, people love talking about good things.

Focus on What You Can Control

You cannot control life. You may work as hard as you desire, but the outcomes are never in your hands. You should strive to focus on what you can control and many times it is your attitude and your actions. You control your actions by deliberately doing things that move you towards your goals. You control your attitude by deciding your mindset. You should always strive to have a positive mindset. A positive mindset means that you have positive expectations towards your future and that you react positively to all people and situations. A positive reaction normally involves choosing to take responsibility and looking for ways to solve the problems that arise instead of complaining.

Develop Self-Discipline

Hard work teaches you discipline. By consistently working on your goals, you train yourself to stick to the plan. You won't always feel like it, but if you have committed to it, then you must do it. This discipline will eventually seep into other areas of your life. Self-discipline is a very important quality to have if you desire success. This is because your goals are yours and no one will push you to go after them. There are some areas that will require your hard work and discipline if you desire success and they are elaborated below.

Napier Clark

You need to have the discipline to manage your time effectively. We all have twenty-four hours in a day, yet you always find people who seem to do more with their day than others. By managing your time, you can dedicate specific amounts of time to the things that you want to accomplish. Time management will also allow you to allocate time to leisure and your relationships. It has the added advantage of allowing you to enjoy that time because you are not worried about unfinished work and unmet deadlines. If you wish to eliminate worry and stress in your life when it comes to work, it is mandatory that you learn how to utilize your time effectively

If you want to produce your best work, you must be ready to develop yourself. Self-development requires self-discipline because it rarely profits anyone but yourself. Furthermore, the process of self-development never ends. You develop yourself through continuous learning. Read books on how to change your outlook, the habits of successful people and how to be a better person.

Besides reading books, it is important to apply what you learn in your life. Install new habits that make you better. A word of caution though, books are written by individuals and they talk about what worked for them. However, no method is one-size-fits-all. If you try something and it does not work, be willing to discard it. In this way, you implement methods that help improve you, and you don't overburden yourself with things that don't work.

Discipline is necessary for financial management. If you desire to be wealthy, you need to leverage your resources and your cash flow so that they can earn for you. This does not necessarily mean that you need to go to school and learn finance. There are many books and seminars that are geared towards teaching individuals to manage their own finances. You can even hire a personal coach to train you. There are, however, some principles that are universal that you should obey. These include:

- Your expenses should never exceed your income. When your expenses exceed what you are earning, you begin to accumulate debt which reduces how much usable income you have and thus begins a vicious cycle.

- You should always save. It is advisable that you save before you begin to spend not save whatever remains.

- Minimize your expenses whenever possible so that you can save. Prioritize on essentials and reward yourself with luxuries and non-essentials.

- Invest your money. When you invest, you can compound your money through interest, therefore making your money earn for you.

- Track your money. This is the best way to be able to identify where your money is going and how you can use it better

- Don't keep all your eggs in one basket. When it comes to investments, diversify your portfolio so that you do not lose all your money if an investment does not work out as expected.

There are many ways to acquire riches. Some are what we call silver bullets; they are shortcuts that promise you that you can get money without having to do any actual work. The main problem is that these methods favor very few people. The other problem is about self-actualization. We value what we work hard for more than what we get for free or what we get for no work. If you desire lasting riches and accomplishment, stop looking for the next best solution to make you money fast. Get creative. Think of a plan that might work, execute it and tackle any challenges you face in order to get success. If you pair this advice with the following pointers, you are well on your way to success.

- Learn the difference between hard work and smart work.

- Learn financial management.

- Learn to be self-disciplined

What silver bullets have you been using in your life trying to get wealth faster? Ask around for the number of people who have gained significant success using those methods. You may be surprised how few they are.

The lottery ticket or any other silver bullet are the irrefutable items that most of us buy in abundance that is a complete waste of money. If you are guilty of investing too much of your time and money on lottery tickets you need to stop, channel that effort and financial investment into something tangible and more pragmatic in order to reach 100% of your true potential.

Now, what plan have you been putting off that you know might work? Start today. You will be surprised where you will be a year from now if you are consistent.

Chapter 3:
The Power of a Goal

A goal is a desired vision and outcome that a person or an organization visualizes, plans for, and commits to achieving. For many people, the only goals they set in their lives are New Year's resolutions which are often discarded by January 15th. If you were to analyses some of the most successful people, however, they will all tell you that their success came as a result of having goals that they actively worked towards. A goal is an external representation of the desires a person has. Setting goals are not hard, but the success that follows executed goals is amazing. Many times, goals are stated in terms of the end results that one desires, for example, one can have a goal to lose weight, to travel, to get a certain result in school or even to purchase an object like a laptop

There are mainly two types of goals, task-based goals, and performance-based goals. A task-based goal is one that focuses on the activities that a person wants to perform or wants to be able to perform at the end of a specified amount of time. Performance-based goals on the other hand focus or what a person desires to achieve at the end of the goal.

It is often better to set task-based goals rather than performance-based goals. This is because you have control over what actions you take, but most of the time, your performance is not something you can control. This is normally the main reason why many New Year resolutions fail. Those who set resolutions to lose weight, for example, find that they have no control over how fast they can shed off the weight. Those who, however, set goals to exercise a certain number of times a week can easily measure if they are failing at their task or not and therefore, they are better able to stick to their goals.

Why You Should Set Goals

You cannot get to any destination if you do not know where it is. Let's say you desire to visit a national park a few states away. This is your goal. When you know where you want to go, you can now buy the correct map, pack the things you need for the trip, set aside the money you think will allow you to make this trip and even organize how you will get to the destination. All these steps arise as a result of knowing your destination. That is the main importance of setting a goal; it clarifies what you will need to do and become in order to achieve your dreams.

There are resources out there that will give you the information you need on how you can set your goals. However, there are a few important things you need to consider when setting your goals.

Your goals should be balanced. You need to set goals that grow and evolve your life completely, not just career or health goals. When people focus on growing aspects of their lives and ignore others, they often find that they end up not being as happy as they would like when they achieve their goals. Take an example of a wealthy lawyer or CEO who went after his career goals at the expense of his wealth and his relationships.

While he may achieve the wealth and career success he desired, he may have no close family or friends to celebrate with and spend his wealth on, or he may be sick and need to channel most of his wealth into medical bills. When you create goals in the categories of your life that are important to you, you can enjoy your life more. In fact, one of the most common regrets of the people on their death beds is that they worked too hard at the expense of their health and relationships. The main categories you can consider when setting your goals are:

- Health and wellbeing
- Family and relationships
- Career and work
- Money and material possessions
- Creativity and experiences

You also need to define your goals and why you want them. Defining your goals is useful in clarifying what it is that you want. When you add why it is that you want this goal, you are better able to distinguish between goals that are worthwhile from those that aren't. The best way to define your goals is by writing them down. You are better able to analyze your goals when they are written down.

This process of writing your goals down allows for reflection and introspection which is very important. It is not uncommon for people to write down their goals and to realize that they are not realistic, that they will not lead to the wealth and success they desire or that they really aren't their goals but other people's visions they took on as their own. Your goals should always be in line with your purpose, your vision and your mission in life.

Break down your goals into actionable plans. When you have your goals written down, you are now able to break them down into steps that you can follow. How do you eat an elephant? One bite at a time. It does not really matter how big your goals are. They just need to be measurable and attainable. In order to make an actionable plan, decide how you will know when your goal is achieved. Then break down how you can get to this point by figuring out your yearly, monthly and weekly milestones. Once you know what you desire to do on a weekly basis, then you can set up daily habits and routines that will support you in attaining your goal. The reason you set daily habits is that they allow you to make daily progress towards your goal and they give you something to commit to.

Set deadlines, track your progress and schedule your time. When you have an end goal in mind, you should also decide on a reasonable deadline. This will help you understand and define your weekly, monthly and yearly milestones. Also setting deadlines allows you to divide your goals into short term goals and long-term goals. Once you know what these are, you can now schedule your time.

Some people do this by deciding a minimum number of hours they wish to work on their goals each week, and some decide to set daily time blocks for their goals. This allows you to come up with routines you can follow daily and weekly so that you meet your milestones. You can only track what you can measure and having this time blocks is a very good way to track your progress. When you can see how far you have come from, you become motivated to keep the momentum and persevere with your goals.

Having goals sometimes requires you to tailor your environment so that it works for you. For example, if you decide that you want to be working on a certain project at a particular time every day, you can find a quiet place to be working from every day and even remove any distractions in that environment so that you work effectively. You can also anticipate your physical needs so that you are always ready for that time. If it is after lunch, for example, you can ensure that you always eat beforehand, you can switch your phone off to reduce distractions, and you can even ask that you are not disturbed during that time as you need to focus. Your environment can assist you in achieving your dreams, or it can lead to senseless distractions which later lead to incomplete milestones.

Importance of Goals

As was mentioned earlier, having a goal is like having a map. Goals give you a sense of direction. They allow you to know what it is that you are required to do and why, so that you can achieve your dreams. Besides this reason, there are other benefits of having goals and the main ones are discussed below.

Goals direct your focus. Many people aimlessly go through life reacting to life's circumstances and never seeing what they can really become. When you have a goal, you can know what is important and what isn't and therefore you are able to be focused. For example, if you decide that your goal is to work several hours a day on creating a business with a friend, you will not spend your time sitting in front of the television when you know that that time can be better spent researching and reading about how to make that business work. You will focus on activities that build your goals.

Goals help in decision making. When you have a goal, you are clear on what it is that you want out of your life. Someone with a goal to live healthy will have an easier time saying no to requests by friends to go out and eat unhealthy foods. When you have decided to take several steps towards your goal, you take a lot of the willpower struggle out of your decision-making process. You have to make many decisions throughout the day, and when you have clear goals, you are working towards, some decisions become easier to make as you can just ask yourself if the decision you are making is in line with your goals or not

Goals can be a substitute for motivation. We do not always feel like doing the things we know we ought to do. Many of the times, the decisions that we must make and the habits we must keep in order to attain our goals won't feel good now. No one feels like exercising all the time, and no one wants to choose reading a business management book over the hot new thriller every day. However, when you have set a goal to be healthy, you will be reminded that you are choosing the vegetables and you are reading that business book for the sake of achieving your goal. Review your goals and your milestones daily and you will find it becomes easier and easier to make the hard choice for the sake of your goals even when there is no motivation

Having goals allows you to prioritize your life. When you have goals you are working towards, you are better able to prioritize your actions so that you are productive. As we said earlier, the tasks required in order to achieve your goals don't always feel good. However, when you know why you are doing them, it is easier to make the right decisions. When organizing your day, week or month, you can very easily prioritize the tasks that are important in the achievement of your dreams above those that are just for enjoyment. This does not mean that you don't get to do enjoyable things anymore, but that you can start out your day with the tasks you have to do and have less guilt when you have time to relax and enjoy your day

Goals allow you to build momentum. According to Newton's law of inertia, an object will remain stationary unless acted upon by an unbalanced force. This law can be applied to life and for the pursuit of success. When you have no goals, you may be an object at rest. You will not make any progress towards any dreams you have until you set goals. Your goals are the unbalanced force that will force you to start making progress. Once you are working on your goals, you begin to move towards them, and you will begin to gain momentum. When you begin to see progress, you will not want to stop what you are doing because you will want to see how much more progress you can make. Other benefits of goals include:

- Goals give you hope and confidence that you can achieve what you desire.

- Goals help in beating the habit of procrastination.

- Goals lead you towards self-mastery and the fulfillment of your potential.

- Goals clarify what it is that you really want in your life.

- Goals teach you how to discipline and regulate yourself.

- Goals help in building positive habits.

- Goals help in improving your life as progress in one area encourages progress in other areas.

If you desire to make any worthwhile progress in your life, it is important that you define your goals in this area and come up with actionable steps you can take to achieve them. Success never happens by accident, and you must be deliberate in your life so that you can be successful. The first step is to set your goals. They will give you a sense of focus and direction that will increase your chances of success. Be ready to become the kind of person that can achieve that goal by taking deliberate action.

What do you want to happen in your life? Write it down in a task-oriented manner and break it down so that you can understand what you need to do to achieve it.

Chapter 4:
No Plan B, Only Plan A

Many people grow up knowing that it is important to have a backup plan. Some people use the advice to not put all their eggs in one basket as an excuse to come up with a backup plan, but new research in psychology and motivation is proving that this may not be the best advice when it comes to goal setting. The main reason for this is because it entertains the idea that you may fail. It allows for this possibility, and therefore it increases your chances of failure. There are many reasons why it is always better to just focus on one plan, and we shall elaborate on some of them here

It increases your focus. Imagine you have a plan to start a business. You, however, are not sure if your business is going to succeed, so you decide to come up with a backup plan just in case. What happens is that you must set up the time to plan for plan B as well as for plan A. This means that you divert part of the attention you would have given to your main plan to this other plan. This is a recipe for disaster because if there is someone else who has the same idea as you do, they will probably start it in a much shorter time than you will, and they will probably be focusing on it more, therefore, increasing their chances of success when compared to you. You are better off working on one plan, executing it then starting the other one later if you still wish to when you can give it all your attention

It increases motivation. A lot of the studies pertaining to why we shouldn't have a plan B always find that those who have a backup plan have less motivation to work on their goals than if they had just one plan. This can easily be explained using a classroom situation. If there are two students in a classroom, one who is from a poor family and who understands that education may be their only way out of poverty and another who is from a rich family and who knows that they will inherit a lot of money as soon as they finish their schoolwork and all they need to do is to get their diploma, who do you think will be more motivated to work hard in school?

The former student, by sheer virtue of having fewer options, will most probably (not always) work harder. Similarly, when you know that you have other options in case the one you are working on fails, you will not have that inner drive and urgency to work on your 'only' option and, therefore you will be less motivated to work hard.

It leads to more disciplined decision making. When you know that the plan you are working on is the only one you have, you are very careful when you make decisions that may affect that plan. You will be less inclined to take unnecessary risks that may lead to failure compared to someone else who knows that failure is not as fatal. You will analyze all the ways a certain opportunity could affect your plan both negatively and positively and pick the option that has the highest chances of succeeding. This discipline is what increases your chance of success.

It increases your willpower. Whenever you decide, you cut off all other options and decide to go in one direction. This means that you do not have to decide what it is that you will be working on at that time, and to make decisions pertaining to two plans when you should be dealing with, just one. This is important for willpower because your ability to make good decisions deteriorates as you make more and more decisions during the day. This is what is referred to as decision fatigue.

When you must make decisions about two plans instead of one, you are very likely to begin taking shortcuts so that you can get over the decision-making process. This can be done by making impulsive decisions or choosing inactivity altogether. If you desire to make the best decisions pertaining to your goals, you are better off working on one at a time

It reduces distractions. Much as we would like to believe that we can multitask, the human brain is best suited to work on one task at a time. When you have two plans, you are inclined to give them equal weight as either one of them could succeed. This means that if you come up with an idea that may work for plan B while working on plan A, you will be inclined to take time and think about it or to at least write it down. You will be pondering on the best way to ensure that they work, meaning you will need to do research on both and find time for both.

Compared to a person who has a singular plan they are executing, you will face more distractions, and you will have to be much disciplined in order to prevent one plan from taking up the time of another. Ditch the distraction of plan B and do one thing at a time and you will find that you make more progress and at a much faster rate

It reduces over analysis and second-guessing. The best example of this would be to compare two types of examinations. There are examinations that have open-ended questions, and there are multiple choice exams. In open-ended examinations, you must come up with a singular answer to the question. However, in multiple choice questions, you often find students second-guessing themselves. Sometimes when you look at the answers, you get that gut feeling of which answer is correct.

After analyzing the other answers offered, you begin to doubt if you really were correct and sometimes you choose a different answer only to later find out that your first instinct was the correct one. While it may seem better to have options, it would have been much better if you had just stuck to your original plan. This holds true when you have more than one plan. It is better to have just one option.

It increases your chances of success. This is true when you look at it from the perspective of your subconscious mind. The subconscious mind manifests your dominant thoughts. If you have a plan B, what you are telling yourself is that you don't think that your first plan will work. While it is quite okay to be afraid and everyone experiences that fear of failure at some point, when you give in to your fear and actually create a second plan, you send a message to yourself that you don't believe that your plan A will work. This will lead to your subconscious mind manifesting the failure you fear. When you ignore the doubt and keep working on your plan, you may fail, but it will not be as a result of a self-fulfilling prophecy. Feel the fear but follow through with your plan anyway and your subconscious mind will lead you to success. Often it is not the realists that succeed in life but the optimists

It makes you accountable for failure. A plan B may also be referred to as an emotional safety net or an escape route. As we mentioned earlier, everyone has that fear of failure. Those who create backup plans, however, forget that sometimes failure is actually a very good motivator. When you fail, you are inclined to analyze what it is that you did wrong and correct it so that you reduce the chances of failing in that way again. However, when you have a plan B, you are refusing to take accountability for any mistakes you may make that can lead to failure. Instead, you may choose to ditch the whole plan and find another one.

Such an attitude normally creates a habit of quitting and leads to very few accomplishments because there are very few things that become a complete success after the first attempt. Failure does not mean that you will not succeed, it just means that you need to review the plan and try again.

The worst thing you can do in the pursuit of your dreams, besides not setting actionable goals would be to give yourself permission to fail. This is what you are doing when you set a plan B. When you set your plan B you are doubting your first instinct you had to pursue plan A and setting an escape plan 'Just in case.' You are, therefore, more likely to fail because of this self-fulfilling prophecy and because of how the subconscious mind works. If you are not ready to go all in on your plan, ditch it and make plan B your plan A but do not let fear of failure and doubts rob you the opportunity to see what you can truly become.

Do you have a plan B? Why do you think your plan A will not work? What can you do to increase your chances of your plan A working? Focus on what you can do to make your plan A work and stop diverting your time and energy into two plans. This will just increase your chances of success.

Chapter 5:
Life's not Fair

Life is not fair, neither is it unfair. It just is. We can accept life as it comes, or we can keep fighting people and circumstances which will only result in frustration and discontentment. It is part of human nature to seek justice and fairness. In fact, when something unfair happens to us, the amygdala, and the primitive part of our brain that results in a fight or flight response is triggered. It results in fear or anger, therefore explaining why we feel these emotions whenever we witness unfair occurrences. It triggers such strong physical and emotional reactions that if one is not conscious, it may lead to actions that you may regret later.

Humans have developed a cortex (the thinking brain) around the amygdala, which should assist in thinking through our reactions before we respond. Neurologically, the thinking brain kicks in a few seconds after the amygdala. Therefore, we should not be too fast to respond with the initial emotions felt but should take time to think through the emotions and come up with a logical course of action.

Generally, people respond to unfairness in three significant ways, either they try to control everything, or they worry excessively about everything or they walk the middle path. Worrying is not bad, but excessive worry or rumination normally drains your energy, increases your anxiety and makes you feel helpless because your focus is on the problem leading to inaction.

On the other hand, control freaks try to control every aspect of the situation micromanaging everyone and everything. This is futile because you cannot control everything. The middle path is the best way whereby worry is your initial reaction, but you follow it up with brainstorming for a solution and then acting in this direction.

Some Things Are Out of Your Control

Much as we would like to believe that we are in control, there are very many things that are out of our control. Generally, the only things we have control over are our actions and our attitudes. Your attitude is a result of your perception. People do not like to feel helpless in situations, and this often results in coping mechanisms to manage the feeling of helplessness. Some of these coping mechanisms are:

- Complaining. This is a very common coping mechanism and is normally used when the person who feels like they have been wronged can't think of a way of solving the problem and therefore looks for reassurance and sometimes pity from others.

- Using drugs. While some people take drugs for recreation purposes, others use them to deal with stress, and to numb emotions, they do not want to feel.

- Binging. From over-eating to over-consumption of media (TV, Social media and books) some people try to cope with stress through overconsumption rather than taking decisive action.

- Blaming and projecting. This is whereby someone decides to give the responsibility of the stress to someone else and to judge them as the guilty party.

- Using excuses. Some people always try to explain away their mistakes as a way of alleviating guilt or blame. It is a way of rationalizing your decisions after you have done them.

While these coping mechanisms may relieve the feeling for some time, they are useless when it comes to solving the problem. That is why some habits are repeated rather than looking for solutions that would solve the problem once and for all. How a person reacts to a problem may be indicative of where their locus of control lies. A person with an internal locus of control does not need the approval of others to feel good about themselves, and therefore they are more willing to accept that they are in the wrong and act.

On the other hand, a person with an external locus of control seeks validation and approval from outside, and therefore, does not like to be in a position where others may view them unfavorably which greatly affects their ability to take responsibility. Blame is the most common coping mechanism.

Why We Try to Control Factors and Place Blame
Projecting or numbing our emotions is often much easier than self-searching and finding blame in our own actions. No one likes to be wrong. We avoid feeling the uncomfortable emotions that accompany being wrong by numbing rather than evaluating what we did and acting to correct ourselves. Blaming and using excuses take the blame from us thereby making us feel good about ourselves. A 50-50 approach can help by accepting that both parties could have a share of the responsibility therefore alleviating part of the guilt without excusing the need for action

We expect life to be fair and when it isn't, we want to find who is guilty and make them pay for it. In a sense, placing blame is a way of punishing the wrong party for what they have done. This makes sense considering we often believe that actions have consequences and we feel that by taking the blame, then we must suffer the consequences of the action. This is the rationalization that often leads to mob justice; an injustice occurs, a group of people get angry and decide to find the cause of their anger so that they can make them pay for their actions.

When you consider that placing blame does not really correct the mistake made as we cannot go back in time, we find it is easier to look for a solution than to take the role of judge and jury. This does not mean that crime should go unpunished, but that the punishment should be left to the authorities not just anyone who feels wronged

When we try to take control and to place blame, we feel safe. When you know who has made a mistake and is to blame, we are able to distinguish who is 'evil' and who is 'good.' This distinction leads us to pick a side, mostly the side that is fair and true. In a way, this makes us feel that we are good people and we are safe because the guilty side is made up of bad people. This distinction is, however, wrong because nobody is perfect and making a mistake won't make you a bad person any more than being on the right side will make you a saint. We should always be objective and not try to bring in our moral judgments when mistakes occur.

Blaming creates biases which affect perceptions. As human beings, we like attributing outcomes to people and things. For many people, they attribute positive outcomes to themselves (internal attributions), and they attribute negative outcomes to external factors (external attributions). For example, passing an exam is attributed to our efforts and failure attributed to an unfair teacher or a hard exam. Another attribution error is moral luck whereby a person is only wrong if their wrong actions lead to negative outcomes.

Therefore, a person who ignores a traffic signal is considered less wrong if they do not cause an accident compared to one who causes an accident. Regardless of fault, however, perception leads us to rigid thinking as you often you find you do not want to listen to the other party. Biases create blindsides in our view and reactions and should be avoided at all costs

Blaming comes from having a perfectionist mindset. This can be greatly attributed to social media as people ruthlessly edit how they appear, so they seem perfect but rarely want to show their struggles. When we blame, we do not want to appear like we make mistakes in front of people because we assume that people will love us more if we are flawless. This is a fallacy because nobody is perfect, and we all make mistakes. We will only experience true connections with other people when we are willing to be our authentic selves and show that we are fallible, and it is okay

Blame excuses us from negative behavior and outcomes. If you fail a certain exam, the easy way out is to blame the teacher, the exam or anything else but yourself. This is because the emotions that are associated with this failure, i.e., frustration and guilt are not easy to bear. However, when you refuse to take responsibility, you also prevent yourself from learning the lesson you were supposed to learn from the situation. After all, it is not failing that is the problem but quitting. Do not let your failures deter you from trying again, be willing to learn the lesson failure is teaching you so that you do not fail in the same way again.

No matter how much we desire to control situations in our lives, we need to understand that there are some aspects of life that we will never be able to control. The following aspects can be considered:

- You cannot control natural disasters and tragedies. It is futile to fight nature and life as you will always lose.

- You cannot control the actions that happened in the past. No amount of wishing, hoping or praying will change past events.

- You cannot guarantee outcomes. You can do your best to try and get the best possible results, but beyond that, you must let them be.

- You cannot change someone's decisions and behaviors. While you can advise them, it is always up to the person to change these things.

Blame Vs. Responsibility

Placing blame is always the easiest way out of a situation. However, it doesn't solve the problem at hand. The best strategy is always to take responsibility, and this is always hard to do. We may break down the word responsibility into two words, ability and response. Responsibility is, therefore, the ability to respond to a situation so unlike blame which is always looking to the past, responsibility is always looking to the future. It is always better to take responsibility because no amount of blame can correct a situation. So rather than ask 'who did this?' or 'why did you do this?' the wiser question is 'what can we do to make this better.' Remember that personal responsibility is a choice. You cannot force it on someone else. There are many benefits to taking responsibility. They include:

- Taking responsibility always leads to fast resolution of problems compared to having to sift through witness accounts to find who is responsible for what.

- Taking responsibility takes away the feeling of helplessness and instead offers us the opportunity to correct the situation.

- Taking responsibility allows us to practice empathy and compassion rather than taking a judgmental stance.

- Taking responsibility puts you firmly in the driver's seat of your life. Rather than letting your emotions and situations control your reactions, you choose to take control of your reactions.

- Taking responsibility allows us to assess ourselves and therefore leads us to learn from our mistakes.

How Can You Take Responsibility?

- Determine the areas of your life that you can control and act on these. Learn to accept the things that you cannot control.

- Remind yourself that outcomes are a result of the event and your response. Learn to recognize and differentiate responses that lead to positive outcomes and those that lead to negative outcomes.

- Learn to differentiate between ruminating and problem-solving. Worry feeds itself, leading to more worry, but problem-solving leads you to solutions and is a more productive use of your time.

- Plan for stress management. Have strategies ready for when you feel stressed so that you know exactly what to do when you feel those uncomfortable emotions rising, for example, positive affirmations.

- Become more aware of your fears and emotions. Sometimes you realize that what you fear will happen when you take responsibility is not as bad as you think, and you can overcome it.

- Concentrate on your circle of influence. Do not get caught up needlessly worrying about things that you know you cannot influence. An example of things you can't influence is natural disasters.

The life you want will come as a result of the choices you make. Don't allow life's circumstances to dictate and control your emotions. Don't give away your power by assigning blame in situations that you can easily take responsibility and resolve. The difference between victims and victors is in how they respond to the challenges they encounter.

Stop blaming life for how your life is because it will never stop to apologize to you or to soothe you. Take the bull by the horns and refuse to be defeated. Learn to take accountability. This does not mean you beat yourself up, but that you ask what is important in that situation and you act.

When things go wrong, are you the type of person to blame God, other people, circumstances or yourself or are you the type to seek solutions? Think of a situation in the past where you rushed to point the blame. Did it make you feel better about the situation? What could you have done that would have made everything feel better?

Chapter 6:
You're Going to Die

One of the hardest things for most people to accept is that they are going to die. This is a reality that many people refuse to consider, and it is mainly because they associate death with fear and pain. Fear because they don't know when they are going to die and how or what exactly is going to happen after they die and pain because they always associate death with loss particularly that of people they love.

However, you find that those who ponder on this fact tend to do more with their lives than those who avoid it because once you accept that at some point you will not be on this planet, you begin to appreciate everyone and every moment and to live your life more deliberately.

The one harsh life lesson you must accept, and which has been accepted by every successful person, is that you will never achieve what you want most in life. Time is finite and you will die before you achieve everything you desire. Make use of the time you must do as much as you can without the temptation to put things off because you think that you will somehow have more time. If you tolerate this kind of mentality, you will never achieve anything, but if you realize that your time on earth is limited, you will act with a sense of urgency.

If you want to know what you want to do with your life, it may do you some good to consider what you would like people to remember you by, what you want to accomplish and what you want to experience before that time. While this does not diminish the fear, it makes you live your life more fully enjoying each moment and experience. You do not have the luxury of time no matter what age you are, and therefore you should strive to live each day as if it were your last— it could be.

Time is a limited precious commodity that is always moving, and you do not get a second chance. This is not a dress rehearsal, go after your dreams, tell people you love them and experience your life to the fullest. Do not let anyone tell you that it is too late to start living the life you want to live because if you are alive, you have the time. Do not put off tomorrow what you could do today.

If you wish to live your life to the fullest of your capabilities, the best place to start would be to learn time management. Time management is the deliberate planning and utilization of one's time to the best of one's ability. It is through time management that you can accomplish even your wildest dreams while still setting aside time to enjoy and have good experiences with family and friends. This life is not all about work and money, and you will find true fulfillment when you are able to make time for the things that are important to you while still going after your goals and aspirations.

Why Manage Your Time

- You need to manage our time because your time here is finite. By managing your time, you will be able to accomplish more in the time you have.

- Managing your time helps you to accomplish more things in a shorter time.

- Managing your time improves decision making as you make decisions based on how they affect your goals and your schedule.

- Managing your time increases opportunities to learn and explore as you can actively plan for them.

- Managing your time increases your chances of success as you can set routines, activities, and habits that support your goals.

- Managing your time reduces stress and overwhelm as you can plan for any tasks you have and do them before they are due.

- Managing your time teaches you discipline, particularly if you can stick to your time management plan.

- Managing your time allows you to enjoy your free time as you fit in your work during your work periods and leave out time for other things.

How to Manage Your Time

There are many time managements resources out there, but there are some universal principles of time management, and we shall discuss some of them. The best results from time management can be achieved when you take some time to track what you do so that you know how you are currently spending your time. Knowledge is power, and this knowledge will allow you to understand your natural body rhythms (when you are most active) if you have activities that occur on a daily basis and how long they take as well as understanding activities in your life that serve no purpose and need to be eliminated.

If there is something you need to do, write it down. The human brain is limited in how many things it can keep in its short-term memory bank in terms of things you say you will remember, and activities of the day could very easily overwhelm you such that you forget some of them. Some people prefer to keep a master task list that contains all the things they want to get done. Later, when you are creating daily or weekly plans, you can refer to your task list and distribute the tasks without any hustle.

There is an ongoing debate about whether a daily planner is more effective than a weekly planner. A weekly planner allows you to assign certain activities to days. For example, you could assign any creative tasks to Mondays, Wednesdays, and Fridays, allocate meetings to Tuesdays and Thursdays, assign Saturdays for fun and Sundays for planning. On the other hand, you could also assign specific hours to these tasks throughout your day, for example, mornings for creative work and afternoons for meetings and evenings for spontaneous activities. Whichever one you decide, pick one, test it out and when it doesn't work, discard and try another one.

Learn to prioritize your tasks. The best way to do this would be to use the 80/20 principle. This principle states that 80 percent of the outcomes normally come from 20 percent of effort. The percentage may fluctuate, but it is generally accepted that there are some activities that carry more weight than others. You need to find out the activities that carry the most weight and work on them first because they normally require the most effort.

Many times, you will find that by carrying out these activities first, you may eliminate the need for some of the smaller tasks or you may save them for a time when you are feeling less motivated and are more tired. Prioritization shall be expounded on more a little later in the chapter.

You need to learn to delegate. There are some things that you can do that someone else can do faster and more effectively. When you spend your time doing all the activities in your task list, you find that you get exhausted very fast and that you do not have enough, time to do the more important tasks. Some people fear delegating because they are perfectionists and often hold the view that no one can do the task as well as they can, but this is a recipe for disaster. If you want your task done in a specific way, feel free to give detailed instructions, assign the job to someone who you know can do the task well and use that time to work on other things. Delegating also works for tasks that you do not like doing, but that you can let another person do.

Avoid multitasking at all costs. You may be tempted to multitask thinking that you will accomplish the job faster. While this may be true, you often find that you do not perform the task as well as you could have had you taken the time to focus on one task at a time. When you concentrate on one task at a time, you can easily get into flow state which is where new ideas come from and which has been shown to increase the speed of learning and comprehension. Set specific times for working on a task, then commit to doing that task until it is done or until the time is up.

Avoid over-planning. Your day will rarely go exactly as you planned it. You need to schedule in time for distractions and interruptions. Your boss may give you a job to do, or a client may come in, and you find that you cannot do a certain task at the time you said you would. This is what the time you left unplanned for is for. It is also advisable that you assign only 1-3 important tasks per day. This is important because it ensures you give them your maximum effort and attention and it reduces the feeling of overwhelm you get when you have a long to-do list. You would rather go adding tasks to your to-do list from your master list as you complete them. Don't forget to plan for leisure and relaxation.

Develop A Sense of Urgency

When you have decided on how you will organize your tasks and the best time management strategy for you, it is best to create a sense of urgency in achieving your goals. The main reason is that you do not know how much time you have left, and the second reason is that it will give you motivation. A sense of urgency also helps in fostering creativity and innovation as you try to figure out which strategies will assist you to complete your goal faster. Furthermore, a sense of urgency will boost your productivity, therefore creating momentum. Developing a sense of urgency will require you to be proactive in pursuing your dreams. The following strategies can help you to create a sense of urgency.

- Break down your goals into short term and long-term milestones and set deadlines so that you can know when you are on track.

- Develop a competitive spirit. When you know that there are other entrepreneurs that are pursuing similar goals, you become more willing to put in the work to become better than them.

- You can set your own deadlines. A deadline is a good way to beat habits such as procrastination.

- Value your time. When you decide to value each moment, you will be less inclined to engage in useless activities and therefore use your time more wisely.

- Value long term rewards and pleasure over instant gratification. Binge watching your favorite show may feel good now but having a successful business will feel good for a much longer time.

- You can build an inspiring vision that is both motivating and challenging. It is important that your vision is challenging so that you feel accomplished when you achieve it.

- Build momentum. It is always harder to start than it is to maintain the momentum. When you have gained traction, you will want to keep working to make more progress.

Prioritization

When you prioritize, you distinguish between the tasks that need your attention and those that do not. The best way of prioritizing is by considering how important or urgent tasks are. Tasks that are important and urgent are crisis problems and should be handled fast and efficiently. Examples include projects with approaching deadlines. Tasks that are not urgent but are important can be delegated for example doing your laundry or mowing the lawn. A task that is neither urgent nor important, for example, watching television, can be avoided altogether or done last as they are distractions. Your focus should be on tasks that are not urgent but are important. Here you can have your daily tasks related to your goals.

Prioritization allows you to focus your time on the tasks that give you the most progress. People who prioritize their time often find that they accomplish a lot more in less time. Prioritization also means being selective about the people that you stay around. There are people that build you up and some that tear you down and when you prioritize, you will find that you will be much happier and less stressed. Make sure you prioritize work that you love. This is an easy way to beat procrastination because we often procrastinate on tasks that we do not enjoy doing. Be sure that you will have to sacrifice your time and comfort while you are pursuing your goals, but all of this will be worth it when you are successful.

We do not have as much time as we may think we do for the things we want, but this is no reason to despair. Regardless of your age or circumstances, if you begin to manage your time better, you may find you do not need to work for very long to start accomplishing your goals. It may mean that we are busy for some time, but most good things rarely come easy. Be ready to prioritize your activities and to create a sense of urgency if you want to accomplish your goals. We all have the same 24 hours in a day and those who manage theirs well always seem to achieve much more than those who do not.

Napier Clark

Do you have a dream you want to achieve, but that you aren't actively working towards? How can you better manage your schedule so that you are better able to do more? Sometimes it's as simple as maximizing your free time, whether it is five minutes or twenty. Little by little you will find yourself making progress towards your goals.

Chapter 7:
Never Be Satisfied

Success and wealth demand that you should be obsessed with self-improvement- never be satisfied with what you have because if you do, you will stagnate and will not have the drive to achieve more. Obsession with self-development is a healthy trait if you want to be successful and if you do not have it, it is time you developed and nurtured it in you. Success is essentially founded on the desire and willingness to grow and learn continually.

Those who are successful and wealthy perpetually believe that that change is possible even when they do not know how it will happen. Additionally, they believe that there is always something new to learn to make them better in whatever they are doing, whether knowledge or experience to give them an edge and make the more successful. It is this open and success-oriented mindset that provides fertile soil ground for self-improvement, by opening your arms to the life-altering belief in untethered possibilities and self-improvement.

To be carefree and content are bad for a wealth creation because they slow momentum and stifle the killer instinct required for success. You should always set new goals so that you have something new to aim for because human beings are goal-striving organisms and we get the most motivation and satisfaction from the process of pursuing them than we do from achieving them. It is this work ethic and undying hunger for more that will make you successful and wealthy. It should not be grandiose goals; all you need is a series of small goals to keep you focused and moving forward.

The unending hunger for more elevates your brain on a higher level of responsiveness so that you are constantly alive to opportunities that will help you achieve your goals. Self-development makes you want success so that you are compelled to do whatever is necessary to make it happen. An attitude hungry for more enables you to channel your energy and redirect it into growth energy. Think of your pursuits as a focus with purpose—those who are highly successful like you want to go there by wanting to be better and the woke up every morning thinking of how to do that and worked to get there by simply wanting more.

There is a big difference in being successful and staying hungry for success and history is replete with people who were highly successful but could not sustain the drive needed for continued success. They became very successful then disappeared because the lost the hunger- they became content with what they had. The hunger for more begins with passion, but that can only last for so long because the excitement and motivation weaken with time and must be reinvigorated. This is the reason many people find themselves losing interest or quitting, however, those who sustain success have a seemingly endless ability and determination to keep wanting more.

You need the unwavering desire to defy the challenges and keep you going even when get tough. Successful people always want more which gives them the power to overcome fears and failures the fears, the failures, the setbacks and survive the months, years or even decades of unappreciated work. Hunger for more is hard to sustain especially once you achieve success, but there are ways to feed the desire and hunger for more.

How To Stay Hungry And Self-Motivated For Success

Do Not Let Success Get in Your Head
It is very easy to forget the effort and struggle you put in to succeed once you achieve what you want. Very often, people let success get in their head because they forget the reasons, they wanted success in the first place- they show off and gloat in the success and eventually end up static. However, to remain successful and achieve more, you must remain desirous and motivated and the only way to get that is never to let success get the better of your judgment.

It is okay to be proud of your achievements and success but do not let the excitement of the moment prevent your success from working for you. Always remember that achieving success is the easy part, staying hungry after success is the hard bit.

Have the Desire to Learn More

Reading is one of the most powerful success habits and one of the top habits to boost to sustain your motivation and keep you from the illusionary satisfaction of success. The most successful people are ardent readers and so should you if you want to stay hungry. Reading won't just expand your knowledge, but it'll also keep your brain active. By reading, you are taking part in an activity that requires you to constantly process information. And this alone plays a vital role in helping you conceptualize new ideas and insights.

As you read more, you learn about various subjects from different perspectives. This understanding of perspectives goes a long way in making you flexible and open to knowledge. Keep reading and learn everything you can about your field. The more you learn, the better your mind works and the more creative and adaptable you become. The more you read, the more you know and the higher your chances of success.

This is yet another habit that won't just boost your creativity but will also help you move a step forward in achieving a growth mindset. If your mind is thoughtful and your thoughts are intelligent, you'll experience a constant urge to know and learn more. And this is exactly what you need in order to develop a growth mindset. It is your lifelong thirst for knowledge that'll truly fuel your creativity. And when you are d creative, your thoughts are bound to expand.

By taking part in a continuous process of learning, you inadvertently give your mind the much- needed ideas that help you to think better. People become broadminded by cultivating this very habit. They become broadminded as they are open to novel concepts and unique approaches. So, if you have the same goal, it's high time to start.

In order to achieve a growth mindset through creativity, you need to be willing to try unique ideas. You can't achieve this mindset if you end up dismissing everything that is beyond your comfort zone. In order to be successful, you must be open to new ideas and thoughts. So even if you disagree with something/someone, you must give them a chance to express their opinion.

Having the necessary knowledge in different areas of your life will offer you the backdrop for new ideas. At the same time, familiarity with a specific area will give you the necessary insight to work towards innovation in that specific field.

Be A Little Selfish

Staying hungry will require that you be a little selfish and think more of yourself and what is best for you. Set emotions aside and always think and settle for what is going to make you grow. This will mean that occasionally you may make decisions that will disappoint or hurt some people, but it is all good if it will get you ahead. Successful people are always selfish people- selfish for growth not maliciously.

Gratitude: Be Thankful for Everything in Your Life

Gratitude is a key ingredient for success using the principles of the law of attraction; be grateful for what you had, for what you have, for what you are asking for and for what you are going to have. You must be forever grateful for the blessings in your life whether material or immaterial.

Jot down the things you are thankful for and always remember to thank the universe for them; just like you and I are motivated by someone's show of gratitude in appreciation for what you have done for them, so is are the laws of nature. The law of attraction is heightened more when you appreciate what it gives you.

There Is Always Room for Improvement Many people tend to think that you should put in a lot of work at the beginning and sit back to enjoy what you have achieved once you taste success, but that should not be the case. You will be more successful in practicing daily personal development.

You must that whatever you have achieved, or your abilities can be developed and improved. As much as you may not have control of external matters affecting your achievements, you most definitely have influence over the external factors that will determine whether you are successful or not. The path to success or more success is to be able to control your response to situations and to what you already have- it is a deliberate behavior and mindset change to want more.

No matter how much you have made or how much success you have achieved, there is always room to improve. By setting new goals and demanding more from of yourself, you will ignite and release the hunger to be more productive and positive that will give you the ability to get anything you want. The limit is up to you-you are the decider of how much you achieve.

The other reason why you must strive for more is the inescapable fact that the world around you is changing; what was latest in terms of information, technology, demand, etc. yesterday is not necessarily what is relevant today.

To be flexible enough to be able to change with the times and demands of the fluid world around you, because the world is in constant change, you must be willing to learn and must have an internal desire for more. Keep looking for opportunities instead of worrying about the risks or being content with what you have so far. If you can shift your mindset to never be satisfied, you should be able to realize more success.

Chapter 8:
Go Big or Go Home

Take a chance! All life is a chance. The man who goes the furthest is generally the one who is willing to do and dare." – Dale Carnegie

Many people do not sustain success because they are turned off by risks, but the hard things are just that, risks, and require that you should not be afraid to make hard decisions. You must go big or go home for money wealth success mindset because it is what distinguishes long term success from one-off success. Risk takers are much more likely to be successful than those who are afraid to take the jump because they are not limited and are willing to channel their energy to make things happen.

To achieve great things, you must be willing to go outside of your comfort zone to reap the rewards that come from taking risks. Unfortunately, many of us find it difficult to deal with the uncertainty that accompanies risk-taking because they are overwhelmed with the fear and unease of potential failure. The point of risk-taking is not in the outcome but the experiences and lessons from the process. As much as taking risks could lead to failure, it will help you confront your fears.

We always underestimate our ability to handle the consequences of taking risks; therefore, we often let our doubts get the better of us. As a result, we shy away from taking on new challenges or pursuing new opportunities because we don't trust ourselves sufficiently. The consequence is that we end up underutilizing our capacity for risks and thus block off our success.

Sticking with the status quo does not help because the cost of inaction is way greater and leads to deep regret than any failure you may be faced with as you pursue success. Do not delude yourself with the false hope that circumstances will get better without acting nor should you come up with excuses for not making the necessary moves. Playing safe is bad for wealth creation and success because the things that are not working out now will mostly get worse with time. So, learn to overcome the urge to play safe and keep forging ahead.

Successful People Differentiate Themselves by Doing What's Difficult and Taking Risks for Big Rewards

The first step to winning big is to accept the potential for failure and embrace it. Fear has no place in the journey for wealth and success. You may view failure negatively, but it is a great tool for building a success-oriented mindset by exposing us to experiences where we can learn and by making us resilient and strong. If you are truly passionate about your goals and vision, the more the persistence and perseverance to achieve them will grow. Taking risks does not guarantee success every time; however, it guarantees that you will be a better person because of it and will boost your resilience to recover quickly from difficult situations.

Successful people are overconfident because of the lessons learned and the character built from the difficulties they have faced along the way. Take big chances without fearing the outcome- either way, you will learn through the process and build the skills which will improve your chances of achieving future goals. If you ever want to achieve your dreams start taking calculated risks. Risk taking will enrich your life and make your pursuits more rewarding. The benefits of taking risks:

- You are much more likely to have better defined and set goals when you take calculated risks. Risk taking leads to careful thought and compels you to make things work to achieve what you want.

- Risk taking leads to more success than not taking the plunge. By giving your best and put everything you can into reaching a goal, you have a higher likelihood of getting it done.

- Once you are a risk-taker, your mindset will shift from the safe approach to a more success-oriented hungry mindset which will help you to achieve more success. You will boost your self-confidence which will enable you to take on new challenges without doubt or fear. If you are willing to take risks, you will be exposed to new challenges and opportunities which will force you to learn new skills.

- Risk-takers are empowered to establish new mental limits beyond their comfort zone; you will be able to achieve more when you expand your boundaries and comfort zone.

- You become more creative because you commit to solving a problem wholeheartedly despite the challenges thus opening your mind to new ideas.

You Can't Stay in Your Comfort Zone Forever If You Want Success

Goal setting achievement and success requires sacrifices and a shift of some things in your life- if you are not willing to make changes in your life, you cannot be successful at achieving your goals. Clawing on to our comfort zones is probably the biggest hindrance to us achieving what we set out to do. Nobody likes to change and certainly the kind of change that success demands, it will always feel easier to maintain the status quo rather than make the shift to get you to where you dream of being.

Once the comfort zone overpowers us, the inclination is to postpone or forget what we intended to pursue. Before you know it, it is

November, and you have not achieved any of the things you resolved to do at the beginning of the year. Complacency is the main reason for our inclination to remain where we are comfortable, and it is important to break free of them for money wealth and success mindset. You should make whatever adjustments required to help you succeed, focus on the target and not the hardships to get you there.

One of the main reasons why people are afraid to accept new challenges is because they fear the possibilities of failure. All of us aren't strong. So instead of finding opportunity in a challenge, we usually focus on the impact of failure. This mentality is the sole reason why we stumble and stutter before taking on something new. The possibilities of failure weigh us down, so we try avoiding a challenge and instead follow the same path as before. We make inane excuses in order to avoid a challenge. We do everything possible to avoid getting out of our comfort zones.

But staying in a comfort zone solely because of fear isn't as comfortable as you'd assume. By avoiding a specific challenge, you're missing out on the opportunity to learn about yourself and understand your abilities better. You'll feel perennially trapped. It's almost like you're living a life that isn't true to your own potential. Your mind is clouded by thoughts discomfort, unhappiness, anxiety, and a crippling sense that things should be different.

And this is exactly why you need to accept the challenge and try to make the most out of it. In order to lead a life of mindfulness, with a growth mindset, you'll have to accept the new challenges that come your way. After all, it is these challenges that'll give you better opportunities in helping you assume your true self. Yes, you will be afraid. You will fear to step out of your comfort zone. But if you're really looking to grow as an individual, you'll have to rise above this fear, take the challenge, and use it to its maximum potential.

Things You Can Do to Help You Get out of Your Comfort Zone

Identify Your Passion and Purpose

Before you embark on setting any goals, you need to find a purpose for your life on which to align and use as the basis of your goals and pursuits. For you to be fulfilled and enjoy what you are doing or relish pursuing your goals, it is critical that you first find your true passion and purpose. When you do not have a purpose for your life on which to base your desires and goals, you basically lack the compass to guide you through life, and you may end up not being motivated enough to pursue the goals you have set for yourself.

Your purpose determines why you want to pursue the goals you set for yourself so that you are fulfilled in the end.

Finding and acknowledging life's purpose is the most important thing you can do and is the main difference between success and failure. When we fall short of our goals, in most cases, we do not have a clear purpose for which we are doing the things we do to inculcate a sense of urgency or ownership of what we are doing. Without a purpose, it does not really matter whether you succeed or not.

A clear purpose will help you to understand what you want and then drive you to pursue it enthusiastically and passionately. Finding a purpose for some people is very easy because they are born with clear talents which can be developed, nurtured and pursued while for others, it is not so easy to pinpoint where their passion lies and will need some soul searching to settle on a purpose.

Your purpose should be something you are passionate about. The first step in finding your purpose is to do a self-assessment to find out what you want to do with your life.

Positive Affirmations

Dr. Wayne Dyer says- "You do not attract what you want, you attract what you are." Take a minute to think about it. If you are unhappy, even if you strive to attract happiness it will not happen, you must be happy in thought and mind for you to attract more happiness into your life. Whatever you affirm consciously with complete feelings will give you the emotional experience in your mind. Choose to affirm the good things in your life instead of dwelling on the bad and bask in the joy of living the harmonious and happy life that you are seeking.

You must have a burning desire for what you want, which is only triggered by your thoughts and mind; otherwise, the law will not work for you. Let your passion for the life or things you want to be unstoppable; think about it every day until it turns into a burning desire! For you to continually and positively think about your desires, employ the use of autosuggestions and affirmation techniques. Autosuggestions are the means by which we sway our subconscious mind to enable the manifestation of our desires; jot down your powerful affirmations and go through them regularly. A positive affirmation will be something like:

"I believe that I will get everything I want, and I know that I will get all I ask for. I know it!"

Affirmations and autosuggestions act by convincing your subconscious mind that they are the ultimate truth which strengthens your faith further. These are probably the biggest weapons you can have when it comes to cultivating constant positive thoughts. You must know that your mind is a bank for thoughts; if you have positive thoughts, good feelings grow while with negative thoughts, the contrary is true. Negative thoughts will drain your mental bank of the positivity that was deposited there leaving you burdened by negative energy and despair.

Set and Review Goals Regularly to Motivate You

The goals you set for yourself must be those that will motivate you. They must be important to you and your vision, and there must be a value to you in achieving them. The goals you set should be connected to the things which hold a high priority in your life so that you are assured that you will stay focused to achieve them. Without the type of focus triggered by high priority, you may end up with many goals thus lacking enough time to devote to each.

If your interest in the outcome of a goal is limited or the goal is not relevant or necessary in the larger context, the likelihood of being committed to it and staying focused to see it through is greatly diminished. Achieving goals requires a commitment to achieve—to maximize the chances of success, a sense of urgency must be elicited in you. Without a must-do attitude, you risk not doing all that is needed to accomplish the goal.

As you ponder and come up with your goals, ensure that every goal is motivating and write down on paper why the goal is important to you. Goal setting is basically the process of realizing accomplishment, if done correctly, the impact on your success will be very powerful.

Interact with successful people you want to emulate and can be accountable to.

As much as the goals you are pursuing are yours, it is recommended that you share your endeavor and be accountable to someone to ensure that you keep the flames of commitment and persistence alive. This entails sharing your goals and declaring your commitment to someone who is close to you and who supports your intentions like a partner, mentor, parent, etc. It is much easier to keep pursuing our goals when we know that there is someone assessing us or one who will expect a progress report.

When searching for an accountability partner, you should keep in mind that the right person is someone who will challenge, engage and inspire a sense of accomplishment in you to be able to succeed. The ideal person should be one who you admire for his or her accomplishments. Look for your partner through a deliberate effort so that you find the right match for your needs and goals.

The concept of the accountability partner has been with us for ages, and it is not surprising that the most successful people at achieving their goals engage an accountability partner. This person will be your trusted confidant or mentor whom you can trust and will guide you and motivate you to keep on the right track.

Everyone Can Do the Easy Things; Not Many People Can Do the Hard Tasks for Success

Industriousness is an essential ingredient for success and wealth creation and like somebody said, success is the travel partner of hard work, and there are not two ways about it. You must be willing to work hard and to go the extra mile even after success to achieve more to be truly successful and to create the wealth that we all desire.

However, it is not just hard work for the sake of it. It should be that you work hard within a clearly defined action plan with detailed milestones to help you get what you want but to allow for progress monitoring as well. The only way of knowing whether you are succeeding or not is to be able to reliably monitor your effort.

Be passionate about your pursuits and like everything that you do-you have a higher chance of success if you are happy about what you are doing. Everyone can do the easy things, and that is why most of us are yet to reach our full potential and achieve success. The successful people are the ones who do what everyone else does not want to do because it is hard. So, be a hard worker, and you will see your success and wealth creation dreams turn into reality sooner than you know it.

Chapter 9:
Positive Optimism

Optimists are the people who chose to expect the best in life while pessimists expect that things will always go wrong. In other terms, optimists concentrate on the donut while pessimists obsess on the hole. It all comes down to their mindset. Humans are wired to expect and avoid negative outcomes. This is because when we were hunters and gatherers, those who erred on the side of caution were less likely to become prey to wild animals. However, in the modern setting, looking for the negative side of things serves to increase your misery and prevent you from taking new risks.

In this chapter, we shall look at what positive optimism can teach you about the power of a self-made millionaire mindset. You will know why if you project positive thoughts, then anything is possible, so it will really drive you to achieve more. The reason for millionaire success is in their mindset - as millionaires achieve more and more, their thoughts are deliberately more positive and bigger. They think about the potential future which drives their creativity and desire to be creative and successful.

Napier Clark

If you desire to pursue a goal, it is much better to think big. Thinking small prevents you from assessing the possibilities, and we are at an age where entrepreneurs try to outwit each other by providing the best services. There are many reasons why things could go wrong, but there is always the possibility that things could work out in your favor and it is up to you to decide which view you prefer. Do not get bogged down by pros and cons lists, looking at the statistics of how many people have failed before you or trying to create realistic expectations, open your mind up to creativity and innovative ideas. Just make sure that you are ready to put in the work to make your ideas a reality.

In many studies about self-made millionaires, it is a common trend to find that many of them knew that they would succeed. They tend to be optimistic and enthusiastic individuals. Some of the richest people of our time became rich by executing ideas that seemed absurd when they were starting out but that later bring them great success. They have very open-minded views to ideas always trying to see how an idea can be implemented in order to work and always brainstorming on problem-solving.

In fact, it is not uncommon to find that when they were starting out, they had more people tell them that their dreams were not realistic, but they were daring enough to start anyway and resilient enough to stick it out through the challenges in order to get to where they are today.

Benefits of Optimism

Optimists are less lonely than pessimists because of their enthusiastic nature. Optimists generally respond enthusiastically to people and situations, and they always look for ways to turn obstacles into steppingstone. This quality is very attractive to people and, therefore optimists always find that they attract many people to them. On the other hand, pessimists always seem to be pushing people away from them leading to social exclusion. This may be explained by the fact that many people view pessimists as having toxic attitudes and prefer to stay away from them. Pessimists can find problems in almost any situation and are often complaining and whining leading to negative attitudes that always bring people down

Optimists enjoy more achievements and success in their lives. This may be explained by the fact that they have positive expectations about the future and because the subconscious mind brings forth our most dominant thoughts, they manifest their success. It may also be because they are expecting success so they become more motivated to work on their goals so that they can make their expectations a reality. A pessimist will find possible problems in any goal and therefore not feel as motivated to work hard as they are expecting to fail anyway. Optimists have also been found to get more job offers and promotions, and the reason may be because they are more likable than pessimists and because they expect to get these jobs and promotions

Napier Clark

Optimists are more resilient when they face problems. This is a very important quality in life and in business because problems are a part of life. The outcome of any situation is always determined by the response of an individual to the negative event. A pessimist will resign themselves to the problem, ruminating and whiling and otherwise justifying their expectations about things going wrong. An optimist, on the other, hand looks for the lesson to be learned in the situation, then begins to find ways to solve the problem or use it to their advantage. They justify the saying that it's not how many times you get knocked down, but how many times you pick yourself up, dust yourself off and try again

Optimism fosters self-confidence. When a person is optimistic, they have hope that their future is going to be bright. If you have a business idea that you want to execute and that you feel optimistic about, you will have confidence in yourself. When you overcome challenges and don't let them bog you down, your self-confidence will increase. On the other hand, pessimists don't always feel confident in themselves or their dreams because they are always expecting things to go wrong and waiting for the other proverbial shoe to drop. It is difficult to feel confident about your future when you expect to fail and as a result pessimist's thoughts are full of fear and trepidation.

Optimism fosters creativity and innovation. People who are optimistic tend to have big dreams that they are hopeful will come true. This leads them to imagine new and inventive ways of making their dreams come true. This innovation is also useful in solving problems because they generally refuse to be defeated by their problems. Pessimists, on the other hand, tend to have a very narrow-minded view of life. They spend a lot of time dreading the outcomes and even more time ruminating on problems when they arise that they rarely allow themselves to see how they could turn those problems into ideas.

Optimists are better at stress management and tend to be healthier. This is because they view problems as opportunities and do not let situations bother them as much as they bother pessimists. In health, it has been found that they enjoy more health because they generally do not expect to get sick, they expect to recover faster when they are sick and seem to have higher pain thresholds than pessimists. It is because of this that medical practitioner's general refrain from performing surgeries on people that are depressed as depressed people have negative expectations. Furthermore, optimists tend to have lower blood pressure. This is because stress increases blood pressure and optimists generally manage their stress better by reacting better to stressful situations.

Optimists take more calculated risks than pessimists. Whenever optimists have an idea, they look for ways to manifest these ideas to reality. This means that they are often more open to new sometimes risky strategies and ideas that they feel increase their chances of success. Pessimists on the other hand already anticipate defeat and often tend to play it safe. Generally, pessimists have been noted to engage in bad risks such as experimenting with drugs and bad behaviors for the immediate thrill that they provide. This may be because pessimism never leads to the production of the feel-good hormones (endorphins, serotonin, and dopamine) released when someone thinks happy thoughts or contemplates a positive outcome, but these risks do.

Optimists tend to take more responsibility for their lives. They take greater measures to improve their circumstances, they are much happier and are better at stress management. This is because they are normally looking forward to the future and rarely ruminate on their past unless they are contemplating what lessons they learned. Pessimists tend to judge their lives based on how their past was and how things 'never seem to work out.' This way of living their lives often makes them feel powerless to change their circumstances leading to negative dispositions. In this sense, pessimists tend to act like the victims in their lives while optimists tend to take charge of their lives.

How to Be More Optimistic

Perhaps the best place to start is to decide to be optimistic. Optimism is an attitude and, as such, it is a choice. Just as one can choose to see how a situation can go wrong, you can choose to concentrate on how the same situation can succeed. You can decide to face each obstacle as a stumbling block, or you can decide to look at each situation as a steppingstone. In the words of Winston Churchill, "The pessimist sees difficulty in every opportunity. The optimist sees opportunity in every difficulty'" Optimism is a choice, and it is entirely up to you

You can learn to be more optimistic by associating with more people who you recognize as optimists and disassociating with pessimists. You are the sum of the people you stay around, and if you become deliberate about the kind of people you let into your circle, you will find that their enthusiasm seeps into your life. Sometimes the people that are pessimistic are your family or your coworkers, and you may not be able to stay away from them completely. In that case, it is advisable that you begin limiting the times you spend with them, and you keep from expressing your ideas to them so that they do not affect your optimism towards these ideas.

You can learn stress management techniques that remind you to keep negative thinking (pessimism) away. Meditation, yoga and deep breathing techniques are some excellent ways to teach your brain to keep calm. They reduce stress in your body by lowering your blood pressure and calming your brain. When you are calmer, you're better able to think of solutions and contemplate deliberate reactions to situations. Another very effective method is using positive affirmations to remind you to keep calm. Examples include 'I can do it,' 'This too shall pass,' and 'I am always calm.' The affirmations can be repeated in front of the mirror, out loud or even silently until you feel calmer

Another easy way to be optimistic is to be conscious of the information you feed yourself. If you want to be more optimistic, you are better off reading motivational books, articles, and messages. You can watch positive videos online or on YouTube, and you can listen to tapes and podcasts by people who have positive attitudes or by listening to upbeat music. It is also advisable that you filter out negative information by not watching the news or reading the newspapers too often. This is because a lot of news today is negatively geared towards raising viewership. If you work in a field that requires you to be updated on the news, you can refrain from reading the news early in the morning or late in the evening as they affect how you start your day and how you sleep respectively.

Exercise is another simple way to be more optimistic. Exercising makes your brain produce feel-good hormones that make you feel happier and more enthusiastic. Regular exercise will keep you feeling happy which is on top of the fact that you will be healthier. When we exercise, we tend to feel good about ourselves and our bodies and this enthusiasm can lead us to work harder so that we can create a better future for ourselves. Couple this with making healthy food choices, sleeping better and drinking more water and you will find yourself more energized and motivated to pursue your dreams.

You should be careful to temper your optimism with action. Positive thinking that is not followed by actual action is actually wishful thinking, and it will get you nowhere. You should also pair your optimism with integrity in that you look for the best outcomes in any situation, but you consider the current facts and situations. You are more trustworthy and respected when you can present the current facts as they are even as you strive towards making a situation better? This is particularly important in business so that you do not seem overconfident and make promises you cannot deliver.

Optimism is a mindset characterized by the ability to envision a future full of possibilities and to work towards that future. If you have goals that you want to pursue, it is important that you believe that you can achieve them. This is because we live in a limitless universe in which almost anything is possible and because it does you no good to be pessimistic. Optimism is a characteristic possessed by most of the richest people in the world. It is a very attractive quality that attracts customers and investors alike and keeps you from despairing when problems arise. Remember that it is easy to be pessimistic, but it is optimism that gets you out of the problem.

When things go wrong as they often do, do you find yourself ruminating on the fact that things went wrong, or do you find yourself asking what you can do to make the situation better. The first reaction is the ultimate sign of pessimism while the second is a sign of optimism. Does the pessimistic thought help the situation in any way?

Chapter 10:
Haters Criticism

If you want to be successful, you must be ready to deal with your hater's criticism because you are bound to face them. You must develop the attitude, mentality, and stomach to handle both positive and negative criticism but especially the negative comments. Success attracts attention and with-it people who will hate you for a variety of reasons, most of which you will not know or even understand. No successful person escapes criticism and neither will you.

Success draws in both admirers and critics. Your haters will be ranting against you because of jealousy or envy, therefore, do not be shocked about it. Be prepared enough to take the criticism and strong enough to work through them and get even more success- the best way of treating criticism is to use it as a motivator to enable you to achieve more. Everywhere you look, especially on social media, successful people are bombarded with harsh and unwarranted criticism.

Now that you are on your way to even more success, it is best that you learn about criticism and prepare to deal with it. As much as it is harsh, criticism is an equally positive tool which you can exploit to boost your personal growth and overall success. Many motivational coaches and speakers will tell you that if you want to achieve great success, you must be willing to be hated. First, you need to understand the people you will be dealing with, the haters.

These are basically people who are angry or venting out their pent-up frustrations, which is a sign of their emotional vulnerability and weakness. Simply put, these are people who do not like you because you have achieved what they want and cannot get.

The question you ought to be asking yourself to evaluate your ability to withstand the potential hate is whether you are willing to be criticized to get what you want. If you want to escape hater's criticism, the sure way of doing it is by doing nothing, and you know too well where that will lead you. The only one who cannot be criticized is one who does nothing. Hater's criticism is the price you pay for success so, do not let the noise of the naysayers get to you, you must be onto something good that is why you are attracting their attention.

Remember, not everyone will share in your happiness, and you should accept this for a money wealth success mindset. The most important thing in dealing with criticism is how you will deal with it- you should use the negative energy as a motivator to drive you to do more or better. Never let criticism and hate deflate your self-confidence and derail you from your goals. Indeed, if you approach hater's criticism as any other feedback you have received before, you will overcome it.

Think about it- what do you use the other feedback you get? Well, you use it to evaluate where you are to help you adjust get you to where you want to get. Approach negative criticism the same way. In fact, it is possible to find some genuinely helpful feedback in hater's comments.

To Be Successful Means Being Different

You are inviting hater's criticism because you are different—you are successful, and you are thinking out of the box. It is this difference, which is attracting the criticism and, ironically, the same thing that has made you as successful as you are. So, embrace the fact that you are unique and are certainly different from those who are not as successful as you. Here are some things that make successful people different from everybody else:

- They concentrate and focus on the purpose for which they are pursuing a goal rather than dwelling on the challenges along the way.

- Your haters are hoping to see you fail and you will have a few setbacks on your way to success and even after succeeding. Success is for those who can pull themselves back up from failure, learn from them and turn the experiences into catalysts for more success.

- Successful people have no place in their lives for satisfaction as you have already learned in chapter 7. Keep asking yourself "What next?" if you want to sustain success. Never allow yourself to be comfortable with what you have.

- Challenges, frustrations, and obstacles are simply viewed as small inconveniences along the way to the big price. Do not allow them to deflate your drive, rather, use them to fuel it.

- Successful people value their dreams deeply that they are not bothered by hater's criticism or do not care to please others.

As much as you may find it difficult to stomach negative criticism, you can use it to strengthen your character and for self-improvement. Like has been said earlier, criticism is a price of your success but do not be afraid of it because it will only make you stronger. Here is how hater's criticism can be beneficial:

Use the Hate to Emotionally Charge
Rather than allowing harsh criticism to make you feel small and worthless turn passion around and use it to positively charge emotionally. Do what you must do to succeed, rise above the hate and use the energy to drive you forward.

Motivate You to Define Your Goal Clearly
Use the hate to help you be clear and better focused on what you want to achieve. Once you define what you want and why you want it, no

amount of criticism can sway you. Use their energy to propel you and forward to achieve your dreams. Show them more success by feeding off their energy.

Keeps You Humble

When you are bombarded with hate and negativity, you will cherish success but will be humbled at the same time by the attention you garner and how many people are watching your success journey. Use this as a motivator and to inspire you to show the haters what they can achieve if they only channeled the energy, they are expending on must better themselves.

Helps You Understand That You Are Getting It Right

Rather than get annoyed and get into verbal sparring with your haters, this can be a lesson in taking the high road and doing what is right. Having haters means you are doing something right and succeeding because you cannot have haters if you are not doing well. What would they be hating you for?

A Lesson in Being More Accepting and Tolerant

Once you have experienced it, you will know how it feels and should not do it to another. More importantly, you can point it out if someone is being hateful and will make you empathetic to others. More importantly, by going through it and overcoming it, you are in the best position to advise and motivate people who are facing a similar situation and are having a difficult time.

Use the Criticism for Self-Evaluation

Sometimes, the criticism is well-founded and even if it is not, spend a bit of time to evaluate yourself against the accusations. Listen to what they are saying, discard the useless comments and embrace the constructive ones. Criticism can make you a better person.

Use Them to Learn How to Deal with Conflict

Hate and negative comments are a good opportunity to learn how to handle conflict—dealing with the challenges of haters teaches you how to handle difficult situations and to navigate conflict.

Anger Management

There is no better platform for learning how to cope with anger that when faced with criticism from your haters. This is the best place to learn to respond calmly or not respond at all when faced with negative comments and to temper your anger.

Ignoring Negativity

One of the habits required for success is a positive mindset. If you are not strong enough to deal with the negativity from your haters, you are basically falling off the positive mindset. Your haters can help you deal with and ignore negative situations to maintain a positive mentality to help you succeed.

Motivation for Success

As already indicated above, you should use the haters to motivate you to fly even higher. There is no better motivation than to use the negativity of the naysayers to drive your determination and persistence to achieve what you want.

To conclude, all you need to do is to keep in mind that hater's criticism is just that- do not give it a lot of premium because it should not keep you from pursuing your goals. Giving in to the whims of your haters or playing into their hands is very easy if you do not keep your guard up and stay focused. You will encounter many hurdles on the journey to success including hate, take it as recognition of your work and a cue to keep working hard. Let hate be the fuel that propels you to greater heights rather than bringing you down.

Chapter 11:
Never Tap Out

The first rule of success is to never tap out no matter what. Quite often, when we are faced with hard times on the journey to success, we are tempted to give up because it is always the easiest option. The pursuit of success is not an easy journey and you must be prepared to fail before you can succeed when things get tough, that is the time to work twice as hard instead of giving up.

We all get the feeling of despair and doubt when things get tough. Whatever goals you want to achieve, big or small, you will face challenging periods where your commitment and motivation will be tested to seemingly impossible limits. This is when self-doubt creeps in, and you start feeling hopeless, but it is important to remember that the tough times are periodical, they never last. When you have a purpose behind your goals and targets, quitting should not be an option. When you believe in your pursuit strongly, you will have the perseverance to overcome the challenges which may prompt you to quit.

The thing with giving in to the temptation to quit is that you will be left wondering for the rest of your life what would have been if you hang in there. If you want to succeed, you must have the heart to persevere and face the most difficult temptations on your journey to success. One thing is for sure; if you quit, you can be sure of not achieving your goals.

Why You Should Never Give Up on Yourself

There is no room for giving up for money wealth success mindset. Giving up is by miles the MAIN reason why most people will not be successful and is the main difference between success and failure!

Interestingly, the opposite is the irrefutable reason why only 1% become extraordinary or successful - they do not tap out! While most of us are left wallowing in regret and lost opportunities, why we never pursued a dream or goal, the 1% who had the courage and mental temerity to deal with challenges and obstacles and keep going enjoy the fruits of money, wealth, and success.

You Are Bigger Than the Temptation to Quit

Your purpose and goals are greater than the temptation to quit. The effort and hard work that you have put into your journey for success are greater than the challenges you are facing. Challenges are temporary, believe in yourself and remember that the tough times do not last forever.

It Is All Mental

The decision to quit or to stay fighting is all about your mindset- failure or success depends on how strong you are mentally to face problems and overcome them.

Success Is Not an Easy Journey
Just to remind you- success is not a bed of roses. It requires hard work and a lot of patience to see through. Be prepared to cope with whatever life throws at you.

Success Is Not Instantaneous
Success is a long patient process. Overnight success is a myth- if you come into the journey for success with the mentality of striking it rich overnight, you are a lot likely to fall off by the wayside. Many people assume that successful people got to where they are overnight, however, if you asked them you will find that their journey to success is replete with failures and setbacks that were only surmounted because of their undeterred desire for success.

You Will Make Quitting A Habit
Give up once, and you will leave behind a trail of half-done, half achieved aspirations and goals. It is very easy to make failure a habit, and like all habits is perfected by repetition.

How to Not Give Up and Stay Motivated
Focus and motivation are important for the pursuit and achievement of goals. In order to stay motivated in the journey to success, you need unwavering dedication to enable you to accomplish the goals

you have set. Because there is no quick solution to achieving goals to fulfill our purpose and vision, it requires continuous work to transform your goal into an accomplishment, which calls for sustained focus. Focus helps you to manifest your goals so that it becomes easier to reach them. Here are some things you can do to sustain your focus and motivation to achieve your goals:

Keep Negative Thoughts at Bay

Negative thoughts are bad for the achievement of goals. Negative thoughts should be kept at bay and must be replaced with thoughts of success and positive affirmations. You cannot possibly succeed at anything if all you think about is negative. Look for positive things and the little successes even during failure.

Know That It Is Okay to Fail

Nobody expects you to be successful all the time and nor should you. Accept and know that it is okay to fail and that you will probably fail a few times in the pursuit of your goals. Your aim should be to do your best in order to achieve your goals. If for whatever reason you do not achieve your set goals consider it a temporary setback and focus on the gains made, however few, and use the lessons learned for future success.

Accept That You Are the One Responsible for Your Success

No excuses or finger pointing success or failure in the pursuit of your goals is your sole responsibility. Once you realize that you have the power to make or break your achievements, you will always be alive to the importance of the process and will ensure that your goals are achieved.

Do Not Be Too Hard on Yourself

There is no place for perfection in the pursuit of money and if you want to succeed. Be your own number one supporter and always encourage yourself to move forward. Beating yourself too hard when you fall short will only undermine your focus and motivation.

Forget the Past

So, you failed to get one of your milestones right or did not meet a deadline- do not let this hang over your shoulder forever and prevent you from going forward in confidence. Challenges are part of the process, get up and keep moving. Bad feelings and memories encourage negative thoughts- it is important to work through shortcomings and do not let the past determine your future.

Focus on The Possible

DO not be unrealistic or overambitious- to sustain your focus, concentrate on the possible. Work on the things that you can do while always evaluating and reminding yourself of your abilities and positive qualities.

Being Consistent

To be consistent means that you must be willing to go all the way to commit and dedicate yourself to acting over the long-term to achieve your goals. It means that you can withstand and overcome distractions to keep your eyes on the price and it comes down to being repetitive; consistency requires that you repeat the same habits over and over until they become second nature because it trains the brain to engage in the ritual that will help you to achieve your goals. It makes it easier for your brain to convert a repeated behavior into a habit if you engage in it every day.

Learn from Your Failures and Get Back Up

Instead of looking at failure as something that is so bad and the end of our pursuits, you need to flip it on its head and treat it as an experience and opportunity for you to learn. Look closely for the lessons that you can learn from your setbacks and use them to boost your pursuit of for success and wealth. Learning from your failures will empower you with the skills to be resilient and face future setbacks. You only fail if you quit, therefore; it goes without saying that if you do not quit failure cannot be a part of your vocabulary. Do not let the fear of failure stop you from pursuing your purpose.

Achieving success is never a smooth journey; you will be met with challenges and obstacles on the way to achieving your goal, and it requires that you are mentally prepared for these eventualities so that you are not driven off course or you are not overwhelmed to the point of quitting. Whatever your goal is, small or a big, you must be prepared that there are times ahead times when you will deal with tough hurdles and even failure but do not give up.

The difference between failure and success for those who are on the journey to success is the mental strength to face and overcome challenges that may arise.

You start by accepting and acknowledging that there will be hurdles along the way to your goal. Therefore, prepare yourself mentally to meet and overcome any obstacles before you start on the journey to success. You should find the means to deal with and overcome any roadblocks. Even though it can be really frustrating at times as you work towards your goals, you need to learn how to encourage yourself despite your trials. Here are ways to help you face goal-setting roadblocks successfully:

Identify Possible Obstacles

One of the things you should do as you embark on the journey to wealth creation is to evaluate your goals for the potential roadblock you may encounter. It is impossible to foresee everything, but there are many hindrances that you can anticipate if you take the time to carefully interrogate the goals you have picked.

As much as we do not want to think about the potential roadblocks, part of effective goal setting planning is to identify potential obstacles and outline ways of dealing and overcoming them. Anticipating problems and identifying them will help you to come up with an action plan that includes putting out the potential fires. Make a list in advance of any potential hurdles you may encounter them create a contingency plan to deal with them. Obstacles are both internal and external, for example, a lack of money is external while fear and self-doubt are internal obstacles.

Recognize The 'False Hope Syndrome'

False hope syndrome is what has been described as setting a goal, being surprised by the effort it requires and giving up on it. People experience false hope when they expect quick results but realize that it will not be the case. Do not get carried away when setting goals, instead, you have to remember to be realistic and that there are goals which take time and will require that you set clear mini-goals and timelines to help you avoid unrealistic expectations and stay focused. Setting small goals and celebrating the small successes can help stay focused by keeping your momentum going.

Treat Challenges as Learning Experiences

It has been shown that people who treat challenges as an opportunity to learn are more likely to have a positive view of their ability to accomplish their goals. To stay focused on the positive side of goal setting, do not beat yourself up over failures but quickly learn from the experience and looking forward to the future. It is not that people who are successful do not face setbacks or have fewer obstacles as compared to those who give up, the only difference is how those who walk out of obstacles positively view the situation.

Do Not Be A Perfectionist

The preoccupation with perfectionism can also distract you and interfere with your focus. Do not hold yourself to unrealistic standards because you will be left feeling like your goals cannot be achieved. Do not push yourself too hard- be compassionate with yourself and always remind yourself that like everyone else you can be faced with challenges and can make mistakes.

Positive thinking is effective at helping people adapt and learn, rather than focus on the negative aspects of mistakes, rather, remind yourself that no matter how unpleasant, every setback is a learning experience.

Stay Passionate
Stay passionate- as simple as that. To maintain the necessary focus on your goals, ensure that you keep the drive and passion burning. Remembering what you are aiming for will help you stay focused for goal setting success despite any prevailing difficulties.

Revise Your Goals
Sometimes all that is requires to stay driven and on track is a revision of your goals. Your goals may need reconfiguration to keep you interested and to set them afresh, include new plans or even do away with some completely.

The question of sustained focus is a question of attitude. With the right attitude, you will have the mental focus to remain alert to the goal setting process and to improve your chances of achieving success.

Napier Clark

The question of how to stay focused and motivated to achieve your goals is simply how you can influence and nurture the right attitude within yourself.

The focus is important for the pursuit and achievement of goals. In order to stay focused throughout the goal setting process, you need unwavering dedication and motivation to enable you to accomplish the goal you have set. Because there is no quick solution to achieving goals to fulfill our purpose and vision, it requires continuous work to transform your goal into an accomplishment, which calls for sustained focus. Focus helps you to manifest your goals so that it becomes easier to reach them.

Focus and motivation are not easy to sustain, yet they are the elements which ensure that you stay the course to achieve your goals successfully. Adapting these tips and many others will help to remind you of the importance of your goals and will help to keep you focused and motivated to succeed so that your vision is realized.

Setbacks are inescapable and must be expected in any endeavor. Roadblocks should not be the end of your goal setting journey and should not be a reason to automatically deter you from your goals. Analyze and find out why you are facing a setback if it is something you can control go ahead and deal with it, if you cannot, find a way around it that will not force you to abandon your dream.

Stay focused by finding new opportunities from the hurdles you face. As you have undoubtedly heard, some of the most successful things were never planned. Persevere by reminding yourself of past successes to lift your spirit and determination. Setbacks should fuel you to strive harder to be successful at your goals. Never tap out.

Chapter 12:
Millionaire Success Hacks

"Opportunity greets everyone at least once or twice in everyone's life, but if opportunity doesn't find you ready to expand and grow, it will come in your front door and leave out the window." – Matt Rushbrook

These are the top hacks used by the most successful people to get them to the top and keep them there. Success requires preparation as much as it demands that you work hard to achieve it. Your thoughts determine how successful you are thus the importance of millionaire success hacks which will basically work on your mindset. Controlling your emotions and thoughts is the beginning of your success.

Time Is Money

Have the most respect for time because like the old proverb goes time is more valuable than the money you want and to create wealth you need to make the best use of the limited time you have. Learn how valuable time is for success and you will be surprised at how much and profoundly you will realize positive change.

Being time conscious is the one money, wealth, and success mindset hack that will instantly create inner drive like no others and make you the hardest worker in the room. Once you are conscious to the ephemeral nature of time and its scarcity, you will commit to get things done now, rather than later.

Successful people have discovered and embraced the importance of time. It is for this reason that people like Bill Gates, Steve Jobs, Jeff Bezos, Mark Zuckerberg and others spent many hours working on their inventions or businesses with urgent commitment and zeal as if they would not get another chance at whatever they were doing.

The importance of time for success and the creation of wealth is closely related to the concept of Time Value of Money (TVM). Investors hold the view that the sooner they make a dollar, the better off they are because they can then invest it to make more money. Similarly, when it comes to achieving success in general, the sooner you can achieve your goals, the faster you will achieve your purpose or goal, which in turn enable you to entrench your success.

Time is a commodity which anyone who is hoping to achieve success cannot afford to waste. Respect and value time for success. Generally, people who waste time do not achieve much of what they aspire to do. As you learn the value of time, you should also get rid of those who waste your time because they will get in the way of you reaching your destiny. Here is what respecting time will do for you:

- Prevent postponing and procrastination: Once you are conscious to the fact that time is money, you will use the time wisely and to do things promptly without delay.

- Make you more effective and productive: Those who value time have a sense of urgency and tend to be more effective and productive because they know that the only time, they have to do whatever they are working on is the time they have designated it. They work faster and are more committed and focused because there may be no other opportunity to do it!

- Better health and wellbeing: Good time management enables you to distribute your tasks and assign time sufficiently to cover all aspects of your life. If you finish today's tasks, you will not have to miss a family lunch or stay late in office tomorrow. You will have enough time for everything thus negating stress and other health debilitating issues caused by poor time management.

There Is Enough Time for Success

There is enough time in a day for you to do everything you want to achieve success if you have everything well planned to help you make good use of it. Never say that you do not have enough time because those who have achieved success have the same time at their disposal as you do, there is no bonus time for successful people- they simply plan better and prioritize their tasks to give them an edge.

Be Mentally Flexible and Open Minded

Nobody is born with all the knowledge they require or use for success- it is all acquired and learned. You must be open minded enough to accept new ideas because it is the only way to develop new skills to help you on the path to success.

Do Not Limit Yourself

You can never truly realize your full potential or achieve any success unless you get rid of limiting beliefs and habits, the subconscious paradigms that have been embedded in your mind. Negative beliefs can limit your potential and prevent you from succeeding. The power of the mind is the gateway to wealth and must never be underestimated.

Get A Mentor

Get a successful mentor to guide you on the journey to making money and wealth and whom you can get advice from and study so that you can apply their teachings for your own success.

Invest in Yourself

Whether in skills, knowledge, information, better health, etc. you must invest in making yourself better wholeheartedly; otherwise, you will not have what is required to help you succeed. Invest your time and money to improve your skills and better your mindset. Every successful person has invested in themselves before they invest in other things.

Decide What You Want, Once Decided Do Not Doubt It

It is vital that you remember that you are dealing with the law of attraction and making requests through your thoughts; you must decide what you want and once you have settled for something, do not second-guess or doubt yourself.

Doubt is the genesis of bad negative thought that is the antithesis of creative thoughts that will lead you to success; be clear and definite for unwavering sends the wrong signals and attracts unwanted results.

Write Down Your Desires or Wants

When you want anything, it is important that you write it down on a piece of paper; putting your thoughts down on paper is the first step to ownership of what you want. By writing your desires down, you have taken the first step in turning your thoughts and mental images into reality- you have started creating!

With writing, always start off with gratitude, e.g. "I am thankful and delighted that the new car I want is already mine……." And always write in the present tense for you want it now, and the universe is giving it to you now.

Actively and Audibly Ask the Universe for It

Once you know what you want and have it down on paper, ask for it. There are many ways that people address this step of the law of attraction, and I believe that prayers are the most common way of asking. You can ask at any time; you do not have to shout it out but say it loud enough for the universe to hear you.

Let the universe know what you want, how you want it, in what quantity, etc. and while requesting for whatever it is that you want, believe it is yours and see it as yours. You can only be given what you ask for.

Believe That You Will Get It; Trust the Universe

Once you have asked for what you want, move on believing and trusting that you have got what you want.

Stop worrying about what you asked for and how you will get it - leave the how to the universe and concentrate on the core principles of belief, trust, and appreciation. Do not run around in your mind anticipating or seeking what you asked for and do not be in a hurry; exercise patience and do not lose hope or be upset if things do not start happening immediately.

Some asks have taken decades to be answered, everything by nature happens time. You should move on in your stride and let the universe do the worrying on your behalf.

Meditation and Visualization

By far, mental relaxation is the easiest and sure way to get mental serenity and clarity which are the precursors to attaining the right frame of mind for success.

You need to take up one of the many forms of meditation that can easily fit into your lifestyle, and that you are comfortable practicing. It is important to remember that not everyone can do any form of meditation; because of age, health conditions, size, etc.

For optimal mind relaxation and rejuvenation, it is recommended that you perform guided meditate for five to ten minutes at a time, in a setting that is quiet and devoid of distractions. Early morning or late-night meditation is appropriate because these are the times that your surroundings are likely to be serene.

Once your mind is serene and clear then you can move on to active visualization; create exact mental images of what you want and go to them every time you go into guided meditation. If you visualize something long enough it will manifest faster.

Pick your object of desire, choose it in your mind to exact details, e.g. a green 4-door Peugeot, visualize it every day and meditate upon it until the day the universe delivers it to you.

Own and Possess
Once you have asked for the job promotion or the new house you desire, you need to put yourself mentally as if you already have it and feel it.

This step is what we commonly refer to our faith; absolute belief in the abstract is what is required here, it is difficult, but it is possible if you train your mind to lead you there. This is the most important of all steps you will read here yet it is also the most elusive.

Smile even if you are not happy and your spirit will inevitably be lifted, and you feel better; use the same principle for all the bigger things you want, and they will come to you. The law starts working here, so you must own and possess what is yours in your mind before it manifests itself for your realization.

Gratitude; Be Thankful for Everything in Your Life

Gratitude is a key ingredient for success using the principles of the law of attraction; be grateful for what you had, for what you have, for what you are asking for and for what you are going to have. You must be forever grateful for the blessings in your life whether material or immaterial.

Jot down the things you are thankful for and always remember to thank the universe for them; just like you and I are motivated by someone's show of gratitude in appreciation for what you have done for them, so is are the laws of nature. The law of attraction is heightened more when you appreciate what it gives you.

Giving gratitude for what you have and what you have accomplished sets the foundation for a positive attitude which enhances commitment. There is always something to be grateful for, however, small. Daily gratitude drives out feelings of failure and self-doubt which are often the catalysts of disengagement and a lack of commitment to our goals. Take a few minutes every day to appreciate your success which will cultivate in you a commitment and desire to succeed.

Think About It More and Think Positively

This is not a contradiction of what we discussed earlier, contrary to worrying; positive thought about what you want is greatly profitable to you. What you think about most is what you attract and what you become, therefore, what better things to think about than positive things you have asked the universe for.

Stop thinking about what you do not want or be bothered by the negative happenings of the past; negativity will beget your negativity.

Your Thoughts Cause Your Feelings and Your Feelings Attract

Having positive inner thoughts for positive and happy outer feelings is important for success; a positive mindset is seldom found in gloom. Your thoughts control your feelings, and that is why it is important that you cultivate, and nurture feel good thoughts and emotions for an upbeat attitude.

Mahatma Gandhi said that what you believe become what you think, your thoughts are your words, your words then become your actions, your actions turn to your habits, your habits become are your values and your values are your destiny.

Be happy, feel excited about life, be passionate about things, laugh, smile and the world will give you the same emotions and outcomes right back.

Begin to Talk About What You Want

Talk about what you want and 'have already got' with others and include them in your dreams. I would recommend sharing with positive people because they will help encourage you on the right path and remind you of the goal in cases where you stray off.

Speak in the undeterred knowledge and belief that what you want is a package in courier on the way to you.

Act Towards What You Want

If you do not work for success you cannot be successful; it is as simple as that. Do not expect that by deciding what you want, writing it down, and simply reclining in a shell and not doing anything is going to get you there—NO WAY.

There is no luck in getting what you want; even those who come by a windfall in the form of lotteries or any other such contests work to get it. Yes, they buy the tickets or take their time and register for the draws. Success is not a miracle, the right mindset is not a miracle, and the law of attraction is certainly not miraculous.

How Goals Help You with Success

Achieving success is only easy once it is done, the journey and certainly, the beginning is never easy. The goal setting process provides one indisputable guiding star for success which is clarity. Goals bring clarity to any action plan for pursuing and achieving any visions we want to realize; you create goals by defining the purpose first. When you have clarity, dealing with and surmounting challenges and obstacles becomes very easy because the objective is clear and set.

In whatever circumstance, if you want to ensure that you fulfill your potential and achieve success, you must have actionable and effective goals which are really the difference from what you dream about and what comes true. Success is not by accident; effective goals are a prerequisite:

Lead to Better Decisions
They help you to have a better understanding of what you are doing and working towards. Goals will slow you down so that you can make the right decisions and react appropriately to get what you want. Goals will help you align with the goals and put you in a comfortable place mentally to work for what you envision- you can better 'see' and consider more options for success. Goals help you to craft a plan for success.

Help You Understand Yourself Better
You can never succeed at anything if you cannot control your emotions to see thing clearly and goals will help you to translate your

feelings into action that are suited to your strengths and temperament. With clear goals, you will make your decisions, not what others want for you. Accept and interrogate your emotions and use them to guide you to success.

Goal setting enables clarity of purpose without which you will be bombarded with ideas, and you will be left drifting aimlessly doing one thing to another without achieving much.

Motivate You to Action

Goals are great motivators to get you pumped up and to work to achieve the vision you have. While motivation by itself will only get you so far, goals, which are essentially daily habits, will ignite the will and drive you to succeed. Wishing for things to happen will never take you where you want to be, only actions can get you the success you want.

Goals provide you with specific actions to take, which come together into an actionable plan for guiding you on what to do and at what point to do it. The real motivator is in knowing the benefits which await you when you meet every goal, which helps you to dig deeper and push through with the plan.

Bestow A Sense of Responsibility

A life without goals is a life without responsibility. Goals make you responsible for your success and the actions you take to get you there. Quite often, when we are not committed to something, we lack the compulsion and motivation needed to see it through. With goal setting, we are responsible for the outcomes we achieve in life and only have ourselves to blame or thank, and many times when we set goals, we realize success.

This will help you to push through. As you get closer to achieving your goal, you can see how far you've come, and you know that it would be a lot easier to keep going than to quit or turn back. The very act of putting your goal into words and getting started can be a great motivator.

Focus on The Trophy

The trophy here is the vision you have for yourself and want to attain. Since time is limited, having effective goals will help you to focus your energies on the things that really matter for your success by picking out what is important and reigning you in to concentrate on them. Goals help you focus on the specific tasks you have set out to do without being distracted or the temptation to postpone, as well as filtering out the extraneous things which do not add any value.

The most important thing to remember in goal setting for success is to never lose sight of your vision in the whole process. Success requires you to chase your dream fearlessly but within the set goals and the broader action plan. In the success equation, goal setting brings about the required focus and motivation and the necessary sense of purpose to help you realize your vision.

Now that you know what a goal is, what it constitutes and what is required to attain it, you are better equipped to get on the journey of goal setting mastery to apply the knowledge to achieve anything you want. All you must do is believe in yourself, make the necessary changes to get your plan moving and improve or even alter your mindset for success. Goal setting is the most important step to a positive mind and a more successful life personally, professionally and in business.

With the correct goal setting process, your goals are clearly defined, the first step to success which leaves you with a strong sense of achievement with every goal you reach and surpass. In the next chapter, we shall investigate the question of why most of us do not achieve the goals we set.

The foregoing millionaire hacks will get you to the right mindset for success. These principles can only work for you if you make them part of your daily life and routine; the same way you must drink water and eat daily is the same way you must use them daily.

Success is achieved by habituation; make these principles your habits to help you achieve the right mindset for success.

Chapter 13:
The Challenge

Throughout this book, you have learned what you need to help you take the right steps towards achieving a money wealth success mindset. The way to success is in the state of your mind—with the right mindset you can achieve any level of success that you desire. You should tirelessly strive to achieve a goal your goals by adapting the information in this book

Like every other skill, success requires learning and practice- you will meet challenges along the way and will make many mistakes as well, but with a good understanding of the process and a well-executed goal setting plan, success is guaranteed. The way to success is simple- do not stop, do not give up.

Importance of Belief

How do you trust wholeheartedly in the goal-setting process and in the attainment of your vision and purpose? Believing in the abstract is probably one of the most difficult steps if not the most difficult in this journey.

Paycheck to Paycheck to Millionaire

You know you want a new car to help you get to work more reliably, once you have the car you can put in more hours at work or even get a second job which translates to more income, when you earn more you will be able to buy the things you want or pay for your college etc. The challenge most of us face is the ability to reconcile the current situation and perceived reality with where they want to be or the reality they want to live.

We are doubters by nature, however, by employing a positive mindset and the law of attraction you initiate the emotional and mental conditioning to drive and work to get you what you want.

It is not for you to know everything, with time the answers will be made clear to you, and you will not only get clarity, but the way to get what you want will be shown to you. The way and the actions to take for you to get to your intended destination will be shown to you, and it will be up to you to notice and take advantage.

One of the powerful ways to exercise belief is to constantly have your goal playing in your mind trust that you will achieve it, create mental pictures of the actual and know that the way will be shown to you. It is like walking into your house at night and flicking the switch to turn on the lights; you 'KNOW' that by doing that the room you are walking into will be illuminated and I doubt that there is any one of us who ever doubts that the light will come on. In fact, we do not think about it- that is the same kind of belief that you need for this process to work for you.

You need to focus your attention on your vision and not your struggles or problems; let your vision lead you to where you want to go. Confidence and belief can only be created and owned by you; be confident and secure in yourself and have an inner abundance of positive thoughts, emotions, and visions for your life. The more positive you feel and believe, the more positive outcomes you are bound to get.

Do not seek anything from outside as all you need is within you; you are the creator of what you want. The universe is only giving you what you create on your own thus the need and importance of seeking within you first. Total belief in what you want and that you will get it is important to realize your desires, without it nothing will work for you. Start building confidence and belief by taking small steps towards total belief, and you will reap the benefits to transform your life beyond what you ever dreamed of.

You must stop worrying about how you will get what you want- that is not your job. Leave the how to the universe and concentrate on the core principles of belief, trust, and appreciation; do not overrun your mind anticipating or seeking what you requested.

Of course, you should not buy into blind belief; your confidence in getting what you want must be accompanied by actions aimed at reaching the desired goal. You cannot pray and sit on your laurels hoping for things to happen miraculously- it is for you to work and create the life that you want

Have unwavering belief in your dreams and in your ability to get them, and you will transform your life like a sculptor working away the unwanted bits to remain with the image he or she wants. So, how do you build the requisite faith to create the harmony you want in your life?

Belief or trust must be fed and nurtured to be able to get the potency and foothold desired; the best way to feed and grow your faith is through meditation and visualization.

Be focused, be positive, and follow a solid routine. Do not let your mind conjure negative images or harbor defeatist beliefs. Instead, teach it to focus on the current moment and on your current goals. Remember, success is about focusing on your present and giving your all to make it better. So, if you're really looking to be successful, be committed, seek knowledge, and make your journey enjoyable.

Nothing about being successful is instantaneous. And this is exactly why you can't expect an overnight change. In order to truly make things work in your favor, you will have to be strong, growth-oriented, and patient. While this might seem like a difficult and infinite journey, in the beginning, it is not quite the case.

Napier Clark

Once you start following the advice in this book guidelines, every new habit you learn will become a part of your success-driven lifestyle. Good luck!

If you find this book helpful in anyway a review to support my endeavors is much appreciated.

Paycheck to Paycheck to Millionaire

Napier Clark

www.ingramcontent.com/pod-product-compliance
Lightning Source LLC
Chambersburg PA
CBHW060453080526
44584CB00015B/1423